The Ernie Hunt Story

JOKER
in the pack

The Ernie Hunt Story

JOKER
in the pack

Chris Westcott

TEMPUS

This book is dedicated to Ernie and Doris, Ernie's mum and dad, and also Aunt Ollie, who all provided unstinting support and encouragement to Ernie throughout their lives.

First published 2004

Tempus Publishing Ltd
The Mill, Brimscombe Port
Stroud, Gloucestershire GL5 2QG
www.tempus-publishing.com

British Library Cataloguing in Publication Data.
A catalogue record for this book is available from the British Library.

ISBN 0 7524 3271 0

Typesetting and origination by Tempus Publishing
Printed and bound in Great Britain

Contents

Acknowledgements

I would like to take this opportunity to thank James Howarth at Tempus for again supporting this publication; Mike Summerbee for his excellent foreword; all Ernie's ex-playing colleagues for their contributions and my wife Linda for again allowing me to 'disappear' for over eight months in order to research and complete the book. But above all Ernie himself, wife Carole and the family. I don't think I have come across such a resiliently cheerful individual as Ernie for many a year and it has been a real pleasure getting to know him and working with him.

While every effort has been made to obtain permission, there may still be cases in which we have failed to trace a copyright owner. The publisher will be happy to correct any omissions in future reprinting.

Note on the Text

The relevant team line-up appears in the text after each major game described.

Foreword
by Mike Summerbee

My first experience of digs was when I left Cheltenham to go to Bristol City. When I joined Swindon Town I stayed with Cecil Green, who was the chief scout then, but ended up as chairman. I was very friendly with Ernie, as we grew up together in the team, and his mum and dad invited me to stay with them when I went to Swindon. Aunt Ollie was about three doors away and they were fantastic people. We lived in the shadow of the factory wall of British Rail. Swindon was quiet then, but when the hooter went 50,000 people walked out of the factory, including Ernie's dad. There was a pub just down the road run by Mr and Mrs Webb, whose son Dave we got to know well – it was a bit like Coronation Street.

Mr Hunt loved birds and used to catch bullfinches and the like on the hawthorns by using 'sticky,' that was his hobby. Hilda was such a lovely lady, she looked after me really well. She worried about Ernie as he was her only son, together with the fact that he was a footballer and might get injured, which is a natural thing, but they worried about me as well. They were like a second mother and father to me and made me feel very welcome, nothing was too much trouble. Hilda and Ern used to go out on a Tuesday or Wednesday to play in a trio at the Stratton pub with Aunt Edie. They played in a group where OAPs could have a dance. Sometimes Ernie and I would call by and join in.

The most important thing for any young lad leaving home was you had to live somewhere that would make you for the future. I would say that the basis of me as a footballer and the success I had came from staying with Mr and Mrs Hunt. They gave me the strength and confidence to carry on and just concentrate on my football. Everything was done for us in a very homely situation and the whole life was superb. They came to the games to support us, including Aunt Ollie, and before the kick-off you could see them standing behind the goal at the Stratton Road end. They were a very close community and the whole family was very proud of Ernie. I stayed with them right through until I was transferred to Manchester City. When Ernie got married and left home it would have been easy for them to ask me to go as well, but I didn't have a house and wasn't married, so they allowed me to stay until I left Swindon Town, about six years in all.

We had great fun. We used to go 'tramping,' which was walking round the town dressed up as tramps. I used to paint for Mr Green, who had a decorating business. Ernie and I went window cleaning, we worked for the corporation cutting the grass and then got our jobs as gravediggers. Of course I got all the tough jobs, like digging the clay graves on my own, while Ernie was wandering around or cutting the grass in some other part of the cemetery. After you'd been up there on your own, every other sound seemed to come from the grave. Ernie used to creep round the graveyard on purpose and come up behind me and drop his shovel! We had to work as our summer wages were next to nothing, but it kept us out of trouble. Some summers I went to see my mum in Torquay and worked on the deckchairs there.

Ernie was very special to Swindon, he was an exceptionally talented player with a great personality. He was the George Best of Swindon and in many ways was a player ahead of his time. He was the greatest half-volleyer of a ball I've ever seen. I'd drive a ball from a corner to the edge of the eighteen-yard box and Ernie would volley it straight in. He was a magnificent volleyer of the ball and could also spin the ball with the outside of his right foot inside the full-back. He played the game easy, was strong and a great passer of the ball, especially for me. I just used to go and knew exactly where the ball would be. We had a great understanding together. He used to call me George – my middle name.

We were on the ground staff together, sweeping the terraces and had some great fun doing that. After the games we had to wait until the other players were out of the bath, then we would have a bath. We would clean the changing rooms and make sure the boots were put to one side for cleaning on the Sunday, even though we were playing regularly in the first team, as we were still doing ground staff duties. I come from a footballing family and I think that basis in life gave us a perfect springboard for our future lives.

Our manager Bert Head believed in young players and when you look back on it, our lifestyle was brilliant. The Swindon days were very special, the football was superb and we were very successful. It was a great upbringing and Bert was a wonderful manager. When we first came through from the Third Division, we had an unbeaten run of nine games against some good teams and some tough players. When we got promotion Manchester City were the first really big club to come down to the County Ground (September 1963) and that game sticks in my mind. There was a crowd of 28,000, we won 3-0 and I scored the first and Ernie got the third goal. We were on an unbelievable run and all the talk locally was about the football club. Maurice Owen and Sam Burton were great, they helped us all the way along the line. Mind you, you had to be very careful when Sam or Maurice were about.

We'd cycle to work. We had a tandem at one time with a bag over the handlebars containing our boots, pads and jockstraps, as we cleaned our own kit. Sam would cycle from his house further down the road. I got my first car at Swindon, a Hillman Minx, and Ernie bought his first one, a Vauxhall 37. Ernie used to have to wear a Wellington on his left foot over his shoe when it rained, as there was a hole in the floor! We went into a joke shop one day and Ernie bought a big furry gorilla's hand, which he stuck on the manual indicator sign. As we went round the corner and he indicated to turn left, he would turn it round in a circle and people would see this gorilla's hand out of the side, and Ernie had a gorilla mask on!

We went out one night in Ernie's Vauxhall to Wootton Bassett for a couple of drinks when he had just passed his test. Dave Webb was in the front seat and I was in the back. The steering was a bit light and driving back we suddenly heard this big bang. We carried on a couple of miles down the road, when a police car came and stopped us. 'Do you mind coming back? There's been an accident.' We went back and saw a caravan with all the side ripped off and bedding hanging out. Ernie had hit it head-on and ripped the side. The driver was crying, 'I've been driving for forty years and I've never had an accident in my life.' The policeman said to Ernie, 'How long have you been driving?' Ernie replied, 'Clean sheet, four days!'

Introduction

The tilt of a West Country burr is unmistakable on the other end of the line. 'Maternity unit,' says Roger Hunt, universally known in football circles as Ernie. The moment you engage in conversation, you are attracted to the warmth and humour of this most engaging personality, one of the game's great extroverts from the sixties and seventies.

Ernie Hunt was a bustling, stocky, bow-legged midfielder with a happy goalscoring knack. His favourite position on the field of play was just behind the striker, which in modern-day terms has become the sinecure of Paul Scholes. Throughout his career his goal ratio was maintained at a hugely impressive rate, top-scoring at his various clubs for several seasons. With Mike Summerbee and a cluster of other youngsters, Ernie put Swindon Town Football Club on the map. He also helped energize Wolverhampton Wanderers' promotion to the First Division and will forever be associated with the audacious 'donkey' free-kick goal for Coventry City, executed with Willie Carr and witnessed by millions on *Match of the Day*. A specialist in the spectacular, his volleying technique was perhaps his greatest asset, but he was also a dead-ball specialist. A skilful ball-player and tireless worker, Ernie was a cool and swift appraiser of the game with a sharp mind, reading opportunity ahead of others. He took the buffeting of defenders and held the ball up neatly with as cushioned a first touch as you are ever likely to see, and his subsequent crisp distribution was another first-class attribute.

A self-confessed womanizer, Ernie was a natural pin-up, reflected in the narration of a BBC film when at Swindon – 'His picture is pinned under the desk-lid of many a Swindon schoolgirl!' When Ernie was not casting his eyes over a young filly, he was displaying one of his myriad personal characteristics, that of a generous, witty, compassionate, perky, carefree, crafty, cheeky, naive, emotional individual, a people's person.

Ernie endeared himself to supporters of his various clubs by entertaining them throughout his career and his overriding objective was to have fun. This remarkable character lived up to that mantra in full, evidenced by a sackful of lively anecdotes in this tome. He was in his element when on club tours and loved every minute of the game. He still enjoys the memories, which he recalls wrapped up in a smile. I have merely attempted, through Ernie's words, to capture the essence and spirit of life and football from his era.

There's no hint of an ego – in short, what you see is what you get. With Ernie there's no holding back on issues ranging from match-fixing allegations that shocked the world of football to a quite appalling driving record, and Ernie candidly explains his experiences. His modest nature and sense of humour have remained undimmed through periods of extraordinary hardship and deprivation since he retired. Ernie will readily acknowledge much of it is self-inflicted, exemplified by his battle against the demons of alcohol, but there's never a dull moment in his life story – read on!

One

Roger Hunt, aka Young Ernie
1943-1957

I was born in Swindon on 17 March 1943 and lived in a terraced house at 40 Redcliffe Street, which is in the Rodbourne part of the town. I was the only child and went to school at Jenning Street Primary, then Even Swindon Junior, and when I was thirteen went back to Jenning Street Secondary School. Although I played cricket in the summer, all I ever wanted to do was play football. I was like a normal child in the street, I wasn't overly ambitious but I made it and the others didn't. I guess I had natural talent. Dead balls and free-kicks were something that came naturally to me. I played football in the street as soon as I got up. My grandad became a professional window fitter as I smashed so many windows with the ball! My dad played football for the local co-operative side, which played on Swindon's County Ground. His claim to fame was that he scored direct from a corner in one match. He said to me, 'You'll never do that' and he was right. He was a character and would always buy me a new pair of football boots for Christmas.

My teacher Ben Hyams was a bit of a comedian and said, 'I hear you play a bit of netball, don't you?' That sticks in my head. If Swindon had a midweek game I used to go with my mum and dad and bunk off school. The morning after one match I handed in a note I'd written myself saying I hadn't been very well. Mr Hyams said, 'Oh, Hunt, what was the game like last night?' I had to go to the front of the class and he went to his desk where he had two plimsoles. I automatically bent over his desk as I knew six of the best were coming!

My father was Ernest Isaac Thomas Andrew Hunt. He was a milkman then a baker. I used to sit in the back of his van and eat all his bread rolls. He went on to work for British Rail in Swindon until he retired. The workers all lined up at the Great Western Railway, to give it its full name, waiting for the factory hooter to go at the end of the day and made a rush for the exit. At the back of our house there was a hole in the wall of the factory, where I often waited for my dad to come out. The workers all made a charge for this small hole every day and often got stuck trying to get out. The whole of Swindon seemed to

Baby Ernie with mother.

Ernie as a toddler.

work for them in those days. His hobby was birds, he had an aviary in the back garden and he was always outside doing something. We kept budgies, canaries and bullfinches, and often went bird-nesting. He got me to climb trees and if there were more than four eggs in a nest, he let me take one. He knew what the egg was and would put it under one of his birds to hatch and they would be cross-bred.

My mother Doris was a housewife. Most people knew her as Hilda. She was a bit of a nervous type, maybe because she never knew what I was going to do next! My mum used to put me on her shoulders and walk me to the Palladium Cinema in Swindon when I was five or six. I remember I had five Woodbines in there when I was about thirteen, which made me ill. That put me off cigarettes for life and I never had another one until I met Davy Jones of the Monkees, but then that was marijuana! Mum and dad used to play in a local band in Swindon called the Richmond Trio. Dad used to play the drums, mum the violin and a friend we called Auntie Edie played the piano. My blind uncle Denis was a pianist and was one of the first winners of Opportunity Knocks. *My Aunt Ollie played the accordion, so the family on my mum's side was very musical.*

When I was about eleven my mum bought me a new pair of Tom Finney boots. They were a red colour, different from other boots, with big hard toe-caps and I was so thrilled with them I took them to bed with me! They must have lasted two or three years – I played with them when we won the League and I still had them when I started playing for Swindon Boys. Maurice Owen was my idol, but I also looked up to Tom Finney and it was an unbelievable honour as a teenager to play with both of them in Maurice's testimonial

The Richmond Trio – from left: 'Auntie' Edie on the piano, Ernie's mum Doris on the violin and dad Ernie senior on the drums.

game. I watched Swindon from behind the goal for ninepence with my dad and remember Maurice scoring loads of goals with his head.

When I was about twelve I had too many upper teeth, so had two extracted. Then my mum and dad got me two false teeth and when I was playing for the school team my mum used to say to me, 'Make sure you take your teeth out.' This carried on even when I was playing for Swindon. Before kick-off during the kickabout I had to kick the ball past the post deliberately and run behind the goal at Swindon, where mum and dad were standing, open my mouth and prove to them I had taken my false teeth out! I dared not get injured, as my Auntie Ollie would run on the pitch to make sure I was all right. My Auntie, Mrs Hedges, was a real character, she was lovely, as are my cousins Sandra and Brian. Auntie lived only three doors away – when she died it broke my heart. Perhaps some of my humour came from her. My mum and dad watched all my games right through from Swindon Schoolboys. Their encouragement was marvellous for me. They both passed away in their eighties, dad was eighty-seven and mum about eighty.

I was captain of our school football team at twelve and Mr Davies, who was the Head at Even Swindon School, also made me head boy. We played about a dozen other school sides and won the League. Mr Davies was a director at Swindon and that led to me playing for Swindon Schoolboys. I left school at fifteen without any qualifications at all, apart from being a decent footballer.

I was actually born Roger Patrick Hunt, but changed my name to Ernie when I left school. I went round with my dad quite a bit – he used to ride a bike for a local speedway team and I was the mascot. All his mates used to say, 'Here comes little Ernie' or 'Young Ernie,' and it stuck. It had nothing to do with avoiding confusion with Liverpool's Roger Hunt. Every summer we went to St Ives for a fortnight's holiday organized by British Railways. They had to shut the factory down, it felt like all Swindon went down there. It took about eight hours to get there on the train and I remember kickabouts on the beach and watching dad play for BR against St Ives in the annual cricket match.

By the time I was thirteen I was working behind the bar in a pub. All the older blokes from the pub used to go down to the Mannington Recreation park for a game of football on a Sunday afternoon, where I came across Ray Barlow, the old West Brom left half. He grabbed hold of me one day and said I would make it as a pro. He was a Swindon man, a lovely bloke and still a professional at the time. People said I was an old head on young shoulders. I think that came by playing with adults like Ray, Wac Penny, a really good player and Stan Tuck, and by serving in a pub and meeting older blokes all the time. I carried on going down there on Sundays when I was a pro, but Bert Head didn't know about it, otherwise he would have had a fit.

Jennings Street School team *c*.1955. Ernie is fourth from the right in the middle row. Keith Colsell, who also played for Swindon, is sixth from the left of the front row.

Ernie's proud mother and father.

When I was about fourteen and standing behind the goal I asked a player for his autograph. He said, 'No, I don't sign autographs.' I was really upset and it knocked me back a bit. It did teach me though to sign autographs for all the kids, even if it made me late to get to the dressing room. If people pay money to see you play, then I thought it only right I should sign their autographs.

Ernie's potential was undoubted at an early stage and he played his first representative game at inside right for Swindon Schoolboys in September 1956 at the tender age of thirteen. Cliff Jackson bagged a hat-trick in the 6-2 win over Cardiff in the Cabot Cup. Ernie scored his first goal the following week in a 6-1 rout of High Wycombe. At the age of fourteen he notched a brilliant first-half hat-trick in a 5-2 replay win over Aldershot to take Swindon Boys into the last thirty-two of the English Schools' Trophy. The first encounter was abandoned by the referee fifteen minutes from time when the Aldershot trainer came onto the pitch to attend an injured player without permission! Swindon Boys were eventually knocked out 5-2 by West Ham Boys in January 1957 at Upton Park in the sixth-round replay, after drawing 1-1 at home.

1957 – An early photograph of Ernie representing the Swindon Schoolboys side that drew 1-1 with Bristol Boys at the County Ground in the Cabot Cup. From left to right, back row: York, Price, Pound, Perkins, Notton, Findlay. Front row; Kilby, Hunt, Sainsbury, Jackson, Southam.

In May 1957 Ernie completed another hat-trick with a sublime strike towards the end of the game, which enabled Swindon to defeat Oxford 3-2 in the second leg of the final of the Berks, Bucks and Oxon Cup at the County Ground, Swindon. Being a reversal of the scoreline in the first tie at Oxford, each side held the trophy for six months. They also became joint holders of the Cabot Cup with Bristol when overcoming Newport 4-3. Swindon and Bristol each won three matches and drew 1-1 against each other. The following week Swindon Boys ran out 6-1 winners against Oxford Boys in the first leg of the Berks, Bucks and Oxon Senior Cup competition at the County Ground. Ernie scored twice, one a penalty and the second a header. He found the back of the net again in the second leg when defeated 5-4, but Swindon retained the trophy with an aggregate 10-6 win. As Ernie was classed as a junior, he was still eligible to play the following season, when he captained the side.

Ernie's extrovert nature was already being fine-tuned with a club trip to Butlins:

I first came across Terry Venables at Bognor Regis when I was about fourteen and went there with Swindon Boys for a holiday. He was miming The

1959 – Ernie (on right) at Butlins, Bognor Regis in a knobbly knees competition.

19

Laughing Policeman *in a talent competition, he was so funny. I played in a skiffle group strumming a guitar and singing, but we were no match for him. I would put one leg on a tea chest and played a double-bass, which was basically a broom handle and a bit of string, all pretty basic, but we moved on from there. I liked the music of Lonnie Donegan in those days, the king of skiffle, and later on enjoyed listening and singing to Andy Williams, Tony Bennett and Frank Sinatra.*

In March 1957 Ernie scored for Berks, Bucks and Oxon Schoolboys in a 3-1 win against Kent in the London and Home Counties Cup at Catford Stadium. Inter-county games were viewed as the ideal platform for youngsters to demonstrate their skills in front of the English Schoolboys' selectors. Another goalscorer was Cliff Jackson, who was subsequently selected for England Schoolboys. Ernie also played for Wiltshire Boys and in October 1957 the *Daily Mirror* junior soccer column highlighted him as 'a fourteen-year-old inside-forward who looks certain to hit the headlines one day.'

Swindon Schoolboys manager Fred Coleman, who played for Oxford City before the war, said, 'If ever a boy deserved a schoolboy cap it was Ernie.' Ernie was left with the consolation of being considered the best uncapped schoolboy in the country – he never had a trial, the England selectors consistently preferring Peter Thompson.

Fred couldn't understand why I never had a trial for England Schoolboys, which was also upsetting for him. I did get a trial for the England Youth team, which was for under-18s, when I was only fifteen.

Two

Bert's Babes
1958-1960

Diana Dors and railway locomotives were the only nationally famed products of Swindon until Bert Head put the local football club on the map. Even Diana's father, Bert Fluck worked for Great Western Railway. Head had been in the game a long time – since 1934. Fourteen seasons with Torquay United, six years at Bury, two as a player that took him to the age of thirty-eight, then a switch to coach and assistant manager. He was appointed Swindon manager in 1956 and, with Town having to seek re-election to the Football League in 1956 and 1957, and the club's future in jeopardy, they looked to have some hard days and nights ahead of them. Head was given a maximum budget of £1,500 for new players, but eschewed that option in favour of promoting youngsters. 'I decided I could make better players than I could buy for that amount of money,' said Head. 'We started a youth policy in a club that had never really understood the meaning of ground staff youngsters. I looked for ability first, naturally, then character. I liked honest players with big hearts. I preferred to take a boy who had made the county class rather than international. Sometimes I felt the kids got ahead too early, then stopped learning. The boys that came through were those who kept working at their game. When I went from Bury to Swindon, I left behind eighteen home-produced players.'

Head had a passion for team-building so as to liberate talent, and he recognized a precocious prospect in Ernie, who perfectly fitted his template. Head signed him in 1958 as an amateur. The cost? A £10 signing-on fee.

When Swindon started a youth scheme, I thought it was a great chance for me to have a decent game every week, so I went along. Fred Coleman had put in a word for me and they took me on the ground staff when I was fifteen. Joe Mercer at Aston Villa, Nat Lofthouse at Bolton, Bedford Jezzard at Fulham and Jimmy Thompson at Chelsea all wanted to sign me as a schoolboy. Chelsea even offered mum and dad a house in London and a car, but my dad said he couldn't move as he was working for British Rail.

Ernie was one of several players nurtured through the youth ranks under the tuition of Head, who gave him rapid advancement at the homely wooden-hut County Ground. They were tagged 'Bert's Babes' and, while Head's policy received less exposure than the 'Busby Babes' or 'Drake's Ducklings' at Chelsea, it nonetheless proved the catalyst for a significant upturn in the fortunes of the Robins on and off the pitch.

Cliff Jackson was the first ground staff boy at Swindon and played in the first team at seventeen. I thought if he could do that, I must have a decent chance of getting a game early on. I followed him on the ground staff in 1958 and after me it was Mike Summerbee, then Don Rogers. My first contract as an amateur was £4 a week. My dad wanted me to get an apprenticeship, so I spent a month in the afternoons working as an electrician at a shop opposite the ground, but I was knackered after training and used to fall asleep in the shop. It just wasn't me. I became very friendly with Mike. When he left home and joined Swindon, he asked my parents if he could stay with us for a couple of nights – we eventually got rid of him after six years!

I never had any coaching as a youngster. About the only advice I got when I joined Swindon was from Harry Cousins, an ex-pro with the club, who was the first-team trainer. He was a hard bastard, bless his soul, and tried to tell me how to go over the top, just to touch the ball and go through the player! I would never do that anyway. I was playing in the reserves at fifteen with good players like Jimmy Lee, Roger Smart, Dave Corbett, Cliff Jackson, Keith Morgan and Bobby Woodruff.

In September 1958 Ernie had his first taste of Combination Football when Swindon reserves entertained Millwall. According to the *Swindon Evening Advertiser*, 'Hunt showed up with one or two clever pieces of football, but both he and Jackson were rather over-weighted by the big Millwall defenders.' Dave Corbett scored twice as Town ran out 3-1 winners. In November 1958 Ernie enhanced his stock under the floodlights of Upton Park for an England Youth XI against West Ham United Youth. West Ham, fielding four players with first-team experience, established a match-winning lead of five goals inside half an hour and, although England Youth tightened up after reshuffling their side at half-time, it remained a one-sided game and West Ham won 8-1. United's sixteen-year-old Mike Beesley achieved a personal triumph by scoring five of the goals. The *Evening Advertiser* provided a comprehensive critique of Ernie's performance: 'What a great pity it was that Hunt, Town's young ground staff inside-forward, should be prevented from showing his full talents before the England selectors because of the one-sided nature of the game. Hunt, considered by many in his schooldays to be one of the unluckiest of youngsters not to be capped, was unfortunate again in this match because the trial side was so hopelessly outplayed that most of his energies had to be devoted to a defensive role. He had very few opportunities to show what he could do in attack. These difficult circumstances should not damage his prospects however, for he was credited with being the best of the England forwards and had the consolation of being the only member of the inside trio not to be changed at half-time. To emerge as the best under such chaotic circumstances was surely a recommendation in itself. Hunt never lost heart amid all the confusion around him, and on the few occasions when he had a chance to set up counter-attacks he pushed through several beautifully judged passes, which reminded one of Johnny Haynes when he was playing at youth level. In the later stages of Hunt's schools career one official with extensive knowledge of that grade said to me, "I consider him to be the best inside-forward to emerge from school football since Johnny Haynes." Now another observer makes that comparison. Mr Head, who took Hunt to London for the match said, "I too, thought Hunt was the best of the England youth forwards, although the West Ham right half seemed to have been given special instructions to keep right on top of him and tie him down." Swindon have in Hunt a young, but as yet immature, inside-forward for whom a great future is confidently forecast.'

I remember being marked by Eddie Bovington, a hard man who had already played for the West Ham first team and went on to have a decent career with them.

In April 1959 Swindon reserves picked up four Easter points. After defeating Plymouth 2-0 Bert Head remarked, 'Ernie was still going as strong as any player on the field at the finish.' His stamina was astonishing as he was only just sixteen and the Plymouth match was his fourth in five days – two in the 'A' side and two for the reserves. Ernie moved with the confidence of a seasoned performer in a 2-0 Combination win over Reading shortly after, finding gaps in the opposition defence with intelligent passes. He scored Swindon's second on the cusp of half-time, when he astutely anticipated Andy Micklewright's flick and pushed a low drive wide of the diving Dave Meeson.

By the commencement of the 1959/60 season, eight of Swindon's professional staff of thirty-five were aged eighteen or under, and nine were aged twenty-three or under. Ernie was at the time the sole ground staff member, although Bert Head increased the complement later in the season. He was perhaps surprisingly allowed to acquire the services of inside left Jimmy Gauld from Plymouth Argyle for a record transfer fee of £6,000 at the start of the campaign, whose influence on the youngsters couldn't possibly have been the one Head was anticipating.

Left and opposite:
January 1960 –
Ernie enjoys
training at
Swindon with
Mick Woolford.

Ernie continued to blossom in the reserves until Head felt he was ready for his first-team baptism at 16 years, 182 days against Grimsby Town in September 1959. He was the youngest debutant for Swindon, a record he held until it was broken by Paul Rideout in 1980 and missed the record of being the youngest player in League football by about a month. Ernie was among six forwards considered for the Grimsby game, together with Arnold Darcy, Willie Marshall, David Layne, Jimmy Gauld and John Hoskins. In addition, John Richards was unfit, Dave Corbett did not travel and right-back Freddie Thompson couldn't get leave from the Army for the three-day trip. Swindon were sunk without trace 3-0 by the Mariners and escaped lightly against a side whose all-round skill

gave them such a command of the game that only a sound goalkeeping display from Sam Burton prevented a trouncing. The only bright spot was the promise shown by Ernie, who had no idea he was playing until Harry Cousins flung him a pair of shorts in the dressing room. Defying his callow years, he held the ball like a veteran and did well enough for one seasoned Grimsby director to remark he had seldom seen such promise in one so young.

Burton; Chamberlain, Bingley; Morgan, Mellor, Woodruff; Darcy, Hunt, Layne, Gauld, Hoskins.

I found out I was travelling with the squad when I was sweeping the terraces of the North End. Harry Cousins came across to me and said, 'You'd better pack your bags, as you're going up to Grimsby with the first team.' About the only thing I remember about the game was one of their players saying he was going to break both my legs. I said cheekily, 'Not if you can't catch me.' We stayed overnight afterwards in Grimsby as it was a midweek game. Maurice Owen and Sam Burton somehow managed to put a commode under my pillow. They came into my room and shouted, 'Something's happening outside.' I got up, looked out of the window and the police were about. Then I got back into bed, hit my head on the pillow and split my head, I don't know how they managed to do it!

Ernie followed his debut with an assured performance against Halifax in October 1959. Bert Head was fulsome in his praise: 'He's a smasher and that's putting it mildly. I don't think we'll get another like him in twenty years.' Ernie could have scored a hat-trick in the 1-1 draw, but 'blazed away with gay abandon'. Yet such a stellar talent was already imposing himself, with early glimpses of the power, control and vision that were to become part of his all-round game.

Ernie spent the majority of the opening half of the season gaining further experience in the reserves and, shortly after his debut, Mansfield Town reserves were undone by a superb hat-trick from Ernie. The first was a gem inside ninety seconds when Ernie gained possession thirty yards from goal and let loose a right-footer, which flashed into the net before Kirkham sensed the danger. His second lost little in comparison when a through ball in the seventy-seventh minute from Dave Corbett caught the defence square, and Ernie fired a low drive past Kirkham as the 'keeper came off his line. In the eighty-fifth minute Ernie put the seal on victory when he fell on his knees to nod in a centre from Cliff Jackson.

Ernie also had his first encounter with Terry Venables on the football pitch at Stamford Bridge as Town trounced Chelsea reserves, who also included Ron Harris and Peter Brabrook. Bobby Woodruff scored twice, with goals from Roger Smart and Mike Summerbee, by now also on the ground staff. Ernie and Summerbee were 'outstanding in a forward line that moved well and was always dangerous.'

In November 1959 the Wiltshire colt turned in a 'five star performance' with a hat-trick for his county in a 5-4 win over Somerset at Twerton Park, Bath in the second-round tie of the FA County Youth Challenge Cup. Wiltshire fielded eight Swindon Town starlets, such was the success of Head's youth policy. Ernie scored another hat-trick in the 9-3 filleting of Dorset in the semi-final at Weymouth, but was unable to play in the final against Somerset, having by then signed as a professional.

With goals difficult to come by and, in an effort to inject some much needed fire into the attack, Bert Head recalled Ernie and Mike Summerbee to the first team for the home League fixture against Shrewsbury in early March 1960. While Ambler helped himself to two goals for the Shrews, David Layne reduced the deficit when he stabbed the ball into the net as 'keeper Miller failed to clear a free-kick from John Higgins. Two minutes after the interval Layne slammed a spectacular equalizer from twenty-five yards. From that point Swindon became a different side. In the sixty-first minute Ernie shot them ahead when he hammered in his first senior goal, a sharp drive from a rebound, and three minutes later Layne completed his hat-trick from close range. Ernie was delighted to be on the winning side for the first time in five senior outings. He was considered Swindon's most thoughtful and constructive forward in his most promising display thus far. Mike Summerbee, who had made his debut at the end of 1959 at centre forward, was starved of service in his first senior outing on the right wing, but did make good use of what he had, racing through the gears and creating one glorious opening for Layne in the first half.

Less than a week later on his seventeenth birthday, Ernie celebrated by signing professional forms with Mike Summerbee. Summerbee, who was seventeen the previous December, had delayed signing as a pro in order to help Wiltshire reach the County Cup final. They both signed forms on a TWW sports programme.

For my first professional contract I was paid £7 per week and got an extra pound for every thousand in the crowd over 12,000. If it was a good crowd we could get up to £25 per week. When that contract was renewed after twelve months Bert wasn't prepared to increase it. My dad said I wasn't to sign it and Bert came to our house so my dad could talk to him about it. Bert came in at lunchtime while I sat in the other room. As he came out of the room after about ten minutes, he said to me, 'I'll see you on Saturday, Ernie.' 'Right, boss.' 'What did he say?', I asked my dad. 'You'll have to sign it, otherwise they won't play you.' That was my dad, all bravado, and all I wanted was a rise of a pound a week!

On another occasion when Mike and I went in to see Bert to ask for a rise, he said, 'I can't give you a rise, I'll buy you a couple of suits instead.' So he took us into town and bought us a couple of suits from the local tailor. They were grey and didn't fit, but I suppose they were designed to keep us sweet. I don't begrudge the money players get nowadays, but it's got ridiculous. My reward was just playing the game as a job and I've been all over the world because of football. I've met so many friends and all I ever wanted to do was have a bit of fun.

Ernie's first outing as a professional footballer was in a 3-1 victory at Southend on 19 March 1960. David Layne was again in irresistible form, scoring another hat-trick and alongside him Ernie gave an equally satisfying display of a different type. Playing on a firm pitch for the first time in his six senior outings, he probed and switched play at times with a subtlety and precision which made him a perfect foil for the bustling Layne. There was much talk at the time of their potential to develop a finely balanced partnership. On the one hand power play, on the other craft and shrewdness from a lad whose crew-cut youthfulness contrasted with his mature style of play. Some of the tailor-made passes stroked or chipped by Ernie had class shining all over them. He also stood up well to the more arduous grafting side of his duties. It was a constructive and intelligent display and one old Swindon pro, who had been watching Ernie's development closely, remarked perceptively, 'This boy is instinctively doing the right type of things the average player doesn't learn until he has been in the game for a number of seasons.' Ernie was establishing himself in the first team and already attracting attention from other clubs. Leicester manager Matt Gillies watched him against Brentford, as did a Derby County scout.

The penultimate game of the season was a seemingly innocuous trip to Port Vale. Town remained unchanged for the sixth consecutive time and there was

Swindon Town March 1960 – the first traceable photograph of Ernie in the Swindon Town first team. From left to right, back row: Woodruff, Chamberlain, Burton, Morgan, Higgins, Bingley. Front row: Summerbee, Hunt, Layne, Marshall, Darcy.

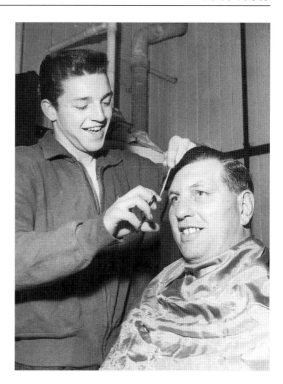

March 1960 – Ernie gives Swindon manager Bert Head a 'short back and sides.'

little in the tame opening minutes to suggest what was in the offing for the fans. However Swindon's porous defence disintegrated when Vale, inspired by thirty-four-year-old outside left Harry Oscroft, scored four times in eight minutes of the first half. Almost all the goals came from crosses from the right, Oscroft helping himself to three and flicking the ball off Peter Chamberlain's legs for an own goal. With Sam Burton horribly exposed, Oscroft scored a fourth in the sixty-fifth minute to complete the rout. Town were described in *The Times* as, 'Thoroughly outplayed in all departments. The defenders rarely showed any signs of forthrightness either in meeting the ball or the man; the wing halves were too often left stranded upfield after moves had broken down and the forwards, although they did not have much constructive support, lacked the mobility and craft of the cohesive, fully supported home attack... Gauld, who earlier had snapped a quick return shot wide of an open goal, forced his way through to score Swindon's eighty-seventh-minute goal. From all aspects it was a pathetic ending to an away programme.'

David Layne, Jimmy Gauld and Jack Fountain fixed the Port Vale game. Our right-back John Higgins heard about it. The winger who John was marking scored the goals. After the game John mentioned it to Bert. John said, 'If anything comes of this, I didn't have anything to do with it.' I thought it was a weird game and Bert, who was sound as a pound, called me in and asked if I knew anything about it. It was a shock to me, I was only a teenager and didn't have a clue what was going on. They fixed other games by approaching teams they didn't think would win. I think they were betting on a football coupon called the (William) Hill treble at odds of 10-1.

Bert Head reported to the board meeting, as a result of which Gauld and Walter Bingley were not retained. It was decided not to interview the players involved in the game, but to leave any further action to the manager. Others had been approached, including Sam Burton and Maurice Owen, but these two principled individuals gave the protagonists short shrift. In any case, both Burton and Owen were shortly due testimonials and would not have wanted to jeopardize their benefits. It would not be unfair to say that the match further hastened the process of the introduction of younger players into the first team.

A sensational trial which shocked the world of football subsequently took place in January 1965. Gauld, the central figure, who was paid £7,000 for exposing match-fixing in the *Sunday People*, was sentenced to four years for fixing a number of matches when at Swindon and later Mansfield Town. Fountain was sentenced to fifteen months for fixing matches involving Swindon and York City, and Layne was sentenced to four months. A case was also made against Bingley, but was unproven and he was never prosecuted. The Port Vale match was the only one implicated during the trial involving Swindon Town. Seven other professionals, including Everton's Tony Kay and England's Peter Swan, were also sentenced to terms of imprisonment.

It was a safe bet that the bigger clubs would soon want to do business with Bert's Babes. At the beginning of May 1960 Spurs manager Bill Nicholson witnessed Ernie and Mike Summerbee in the last game of the season against Coventry City, which Town won 2-0, both goals ironically scored by Jimmy Gauld. Nicholson was sufficiently impressed to ask Bert Head to name his price for the duo. Sheffield Wednesday manager Harry Catterick watched them a fortnight earlier at Mansfield, in all probability the first time Ernie had caught the eye of one of his future managers. Blackpool, Bristol City, Plymouth Argyle, Leicester City and Aston Villa were also said to be in the hunt. Head refused offers of £20,000 for Ernie. 'We will never sell,' he said reaping garlands of praise. 'I rejected a bid from Aston Villa's Joe Mercer only last week. Leicester City have watched Hunt in almost every match this year, but they're all wasting their time. There isn't a cheque big enough to tempt us. He's better than Law, Charlton or anybody you can name. In fact he's the best player I've ever seen!'

The 1959/60 season had been one of inconsistency for Swindon – in October they scored just four goals in seven games and failed to score at all in January. However Ernie had gone from strength to strength in his first campaign, with

16 League appearances and 3 goals to his credit as Swindon finished in sixteenth place. He had learnt quickly, not least how to cope with the banter associated with a group of pros, including two seasoned campaigners.

Sam Burton and Maurice Owen were the comedians in the dressing room, the two biggest characters I ever met. I learnt a lot from them – to be funny but not abuse anyone. They used to set me up and I think I got a lot of my humour from listening and watching their antics.

Sam would do anything for Maurice. We were playing away once and at Paddington Station got on the train, where the carriage was reserved for us. Two blokes were already sitting there, so Maurice said to one of them, 'Sorry, mate, you can't sit there, it's reserved for Swindon Town FC.' He replied, 'We'll sit where we want to.' Sam, who was about six foot three and eighteen stone, said, 'Everything all right Maurice?' 'They think they can sit here.' In a quiet voice Sam said, 'I don't think you can mate.' In one movement he picked them both up by the scruff of the neck, banged their heads together and threw them off the train. There was blood all over the place!

The old dressing room at the County Ground had just one toilet. I was sitting in there one day minding my own business when all of a sudden a little demon, like a banger, was thrown in through the window. It went right between my legs and down the pan, and made a hell of a mess all over the place! I could hear them out there laughing their heads off and knew it had to be Sam. We were staying in Sheffield one Christmas and Maurice and Sam broke open the one-armed bandit in the Grand Hotel. They got hold of this wire and managed to get it to pay out the jackpot – there were pennies everywhere.

Like most of the players, Sam had a bike to get to training and he used to hide our bikes on the roof of the stand. Mike Summerbee and I had a tandem. I usually took the front saddle, as it made me look less like the rear of a pantomime horse, but if it was windy I'd pedal at the back to protect my hairstyle! We bought it for a laugh and I used to hang my boots over the crossbar. One day I got them tangled in the spokes and both of us went flying. I used to cycle three miles on my bike to cut Sam's hair. I also cut an old boy's hair next door to him and then started doing a bit of window cleaning. Every time I went there Sam would put mud on his windows.

Ernie in action for Swindon against Huddersfield Town.

Three

Swindon Starlets Take Shape
1960-1962

Whilst Sheffield Wednesday kept a watchful eye on Ernie's progress, Leicester were the first club to put in an offer during the summer of 1960 with a bid of £15,000. In rejecting the offer Bert Head stated, 'We intend to keep all our boys and build a first-class team of our own.' Spurs also bid £16,000 for Mike Summerbee, an offer similarly declined. Head then turned down an offer from a First Division club of £50,000 for Summerbee, Ernie, Cliff Jackson and Bobby Woodruff. He never divulged the club but Spurs, Fulham, Leicester, West Bromwich Albion and Arsenal had all been watching developments closely. Head continued to enthuse about Ernie, 'This boy has the potential to become a £30,000 player and I only say that because he is so level-headed that it won't put him off his game.'

The shape of the team for the 1960/61 campaign was determined by two pre-season games. In a public trial match the Probables, the older, experienced professionals, were trounced 7-2 by the Possibles, comprising mainly teenagers. After the match Head was asked what he was going to do about it. 'I'm going to sleep on it,' he replied. He decided to replay the match, this time behind closed doors, having warned the Probables they were playing for their places. This time the Possibles delivered 6-2 and Head resolved to persevere with the youngsters. Consequently he chose seven nursery teenagers for the first League game against Halifax – Ernie, Bobby Woodruff, Cliff Jackson, Keith Morgan, Mike Summerbee, Terry Wollen and John Trollope, the latter two making their debuts and forming the youngest ever Football League full-back pairing. The grandad of Bert's Babes was Maurice Owen, now in his thirties and playing centre half for the first time after recovering from a broken leg. Even allowing for Owen, the average age was nineteen. Head's youngsters hatched promisingly with a 1-1 draw in the face of sustained pressure. Ernie scored Town's goal with a penalty and when asked if he was nervous replied, 'No, there's only one way to take a penalty, that's to aim at the iron stanchion!' He did that and scored with a direct hit. It was a reflection of his maturity that the seventeen-year-old had already been entrusted to take spot-kicks.

Swindon Town 1960/61. From left to right, back row: Davies, Mellor, Wollen, Morgan, Cox, Burton, Richardson, Chamberlain, Layne, Woodruff, Marks. Third row: Marshall, Smart, Trollope, Bell, Jackson, Crook, Hunt, Gauld, Woolford, Thompson, Watson. Second row: Cousins (trainer), Corbett, Summerbee, Owen, Morse (Secretary), Head (Manager), Davies (Assistant Secretary), Tilley, Darcy, Morris, Studdard (Coach). Front row: Lloyd, Harber, Colsell, Hellin, Shergold.

The youngest team in the Football League confirmed their potential with a magnificent performance at Bristol City in September 1960. A lightning start by Town brought a goal in the second minute from Ernie. Keith Morgan broke with a run deep into the penalty area before Jantzen Derrick attempted to dispossess him with a sliding tackle. As the ball ran loose, Cook, the 'keeper, hesitated, allowing Morgan to release a short ball to Ernie, who stepped in and hammered it from about ten yards into the roof of the net. The ball lay in Swindon's possession for vast tracts of the match, but they were unable to increase their lead. In the penultimate minute the rookies skidded off the road as a clearance from Sam Burton was deflected to Archie Taylor, who chipped the ball into an unguarded net. Encouraged to breathe with sensible refereeing, this wonderfully clean contest was graced with some fabulous football, the ball moved with bewitching speed and touch over the pristine surface by both teams. Despite the disappointment of the equalizer, Bert Head recalled thirty-five years later that coaxing such football from his young charges was one of the most satisfying displays of his managerial career. 'Both sets of supporters applauded us as we came off the pitch,' he said. 'The fans respected us because we had a team full of kids. They really were kids, some of them were just seventeen-years-old. I had a staff of twenty-four players and only two were not home-bred. Out of the twenty-four, half a dozen or so became household names.' Bill Nicholson was again an interested observer.

The crowd were stimulated as aspiring young locals were given their chance. It also kept the older pros on their toes and made sound financial sense. After a shaky start, the exceptional youngsters settled down to play attractive football, with an entertaining 6-0 home defeat of Port Vale in October arguably the highlight of the season. In an inspired move Bert Head switched Bobby Woodruff from left half to centre forward and Woodruff responded with a superb hat-trick. After Keith Morgan teased an astute pass through to him, Ernie swivelled and curled a left-foot shot round centre half Davies and wide of the grasping fingers of John Poole for Town's third. Dave Corbett and Mike Summerbee completed the rout.

Early in the season Swindon played Shrewsbury Town in the League Cup. After deadlock in the first two fixtures, a second replay was required to separate the teams.

1960 – Ernie and Mike Summerbee pose in front of the Swindon Town team bus.

Above: November 1960 – the Swindon squad outside the County Ground before leaving for Weston-super-Mare, where they trained ahead of the FA Cup tie against Shrewsbury Town. From left to right: Cousins, Morgan, Corbett, Burton, Owen, Layne, Jackson, Trollope, Woodruff, Wollen, Darcy, Hunt, Cox, Summerbee.

Opposite: 1961 – Ernie shows off his ball-juggling skills.

At 0-0 the game went into extra time, when we just wanted to get it over with. In virtually the last minute I was tripped in the penalty area. Either 'Bronco' Layne or I took the penalties – Bronco didn't feel up to taking the penalty so I took it, stubbed my foot and kicked the ground. The ball bobbled into the hands of Mike Gibson, the 'keeper. He threw it out to Jim McLaughlin, an Irish international out on the wing. He hared down the wing, crossed it and big Arthur Rowley headed it home. As I got in after the game Bert said to me, 'Don't worry about it Ernie.' I didn't let it get to me too much, after all I was only playing for seven quid a week!

Town also lost 1-0 to Shrewsbury in the FA Cup, playing them six times that season. Ernie's enthusiasm for the game remained undimmed, although he reflected that life as a footballer was not necessarily as glamorous as one would imagine.

As a professional we spent a lot of time away from our families at Christmas time. One year we were due to play at Halifax on Boxing Day and stayed at

Left and opposite: May 1961 – Ernie's first summer tour. He falls asleep on the boat across the Channel and shares a bicycle with Bobby Woodruff in Amsterdam.

the Grand Hotel in Sheffield on Christmas Day. We got to the ground the next day only to find a load of kids ice-skating on the pitch and the game was called off. Our team bus was an old corporation single-decker with a tea urn in the front with pea soup in it. On the way back we were cutting across country to get back to Swindon when we got caught in a blizzard and the road was blocked. Bert told us to put our football boots and overcoats on, and we got shovels and cleared the road. Bert wanted to go and watch Leicester play nearby. He said, 'Anyone want to watch the game with me?' As it was Christmas, all we wanted to do was to get home. No-one put their hands up and Bert was so upset about that he had us in the next day, training on the pitch which was about six inches deep in snow!

Town enjoyed an undefeated home run of thirteen games at the end of the season, the highlight for Ernie being a brace in a 4-0 victory over Bradford City in March 1961. Mike Summerbee opened the scoring in the first half following an excellent run from Arnold Darcy. Town showed purpose and energy in the

second half and were rewarded with a penalty in the sixty-seventh minute which Ernie converted, having been grounded by Flockett. After seventy-seven minutes a fine low cross from the right by Dave Corbett was controlled by Ernie, who directed it past the 'keeper. Three minutes later Bobby Woodruff headed past Stewart for Town's fourth. Ernie made 46 League appearances, scoring 14 goals as Bert's Babes gained in experience to again finish sixteenth in the Third Division.

At the end of the season Town played four games in Holland on a short tour, enjoying terrific hospitality and making a lot of friends. One match was won, one lost with the other two drawn. Ernie scored (on the pitch) twice; his off-field exploits in Amsterdam are best left to the imagination!

In the summer of 1961 the players enjoyed their annual cricket match against Swindon Cricket Club. Opening the batting, Ernie hit a 'fine undefeated innings of 44, scoring well and delighting the spectators with some fine strokes.' A valuable new acquisition in the drawn game was Don Rogers, a former captain of Somerset Boys' Cricket team.

We played cricket every year against Swindon Cricket Club, whose ground was right next to the County Ground. I carried my bat one match with Peter Chamberlain, who was a good bloke who helped me along when I first came into the reserves. He had a few injuries and seemed to have a cartilage operation every year. I used to say to him, 'How many cartilages have you got in your knees?'

Early in the 1961/62 season Ernie pulled a ligament against Crystal Palace, causing him to miss five games through injury. Swindon's first League win of the campaign coincided with his return from injury at Northampton in September 1961. The two Hunts, Ralph and Ernie, each scored in a 2-1 victory. Ernie's goal came in the opening minute of the second half, when he deftly turned inside the box and cracked the ball low into the corner. A shaky start to the season was reflected in a 6-2 reverse at Barnsley shortly after, but Town bounced back in the next game with their first home League win of the season,

Swindon Town 1961/62. From left to right, back row: Smith, McPherson, Wollen, Teague, Harvey, Burton, Sampson, Chamberlain, Morgan, Woodruff. Third row: Lloyd, Bell, Jones, Smart, Trollope, Summerbee, Jackson, Ralph Hunt, Davies, Shergold. Seated: Hellin, Colsell, Owen, Davies (Assistant Secretary), Head (Manager), Morse (Secretary), Cousins (Trainer), Ernie Hunt, Corbett, Darcy. On ground: Harbour, Powell, Hicks, Peoples, Rogers.

a 4-0 defeat of Lincoln City. After just four minutes Cliff Jackson rose majestically to head home a Dave Corbett cross. Ernie increased the lead in the twenty-second minute with a sharp finish following a through ball from Ken Jones. Any hopes Lincoln had of regrouping were dashed when Ernie fired a second within a minute of the restart. Latching on to another cross from Corbett, starring down the right in the absence of the injured Mike Summerbee, Ernie coolly slotted home past Graves with a low angled drive. Ralph Hunt wrapped up the victory seven minutes from time. Town's defensive frailties were again however exposed in October, when conceding five goals at Bristol City.

In training just before the game Bert wanted to practice free-kicks with me and Bobby Woodruff. I stood over the ball waiting for Bobby, who could really hit a ball, to come in and hit it. Bert had his best shoes and suit on and said, 'This is what I want you to do, hook the ball into the top corner or toe-poke it to Bobby.' He was trying to clip it over himself, but couldn't score. By this time it was also pissing with rain. I said, 'Any chance of me having a go, boss?' He replied, 'No, training's finished,' so we never had a chance to practice it. We went to Bristol and I scored the first time I tried it. It didn't do us any good though, as we lost 5-3.

Town recovered from that defeat to enjoy a fine spell, extending an unbeaten run to ten games with some clinical finishing in a 5-2 home defeat of Brentford in February 1962. With a strong, chilling wind behind them, George Summers put the Bees into a shock lead in the eighth minute. Town's response came in a riveting ten minutes. Inside sixty seconds of the restart Terry Wollen swung a free-kick to the far post, where Bill Atkins nodded it across goal for Jack Smith to crash the ball high into the net. In the thirteenth minute a Mike Summerbee free-kick again found Atkins, who beat 'keeper Gerry Cakebread to the ball. As the ball ran loose Ernie stuck out a leg to divert it into the net – hardly pretty, but they all count. Town's third in the twenty-third minute was the best of the match when Bobby Woodruff found Smith with an inch-perfect pass. The centre forward drew two men before slipping the ball to Eric Weaver, who angled a ball to Ernie on the edge of the box. From twenty yards out Ernie's raking drive flew past Cakebread. Two minutes from the break Atkins surged through the slow-responding defence and planted a right-footed drive into the net for the fourth. George Francis scored a consolation goal for Brentford in the second half before Smith evaded a demoralized defence in the seventy-sixth minute to ram home the fifth from close range.

In March 1962 another goal sourced from a dead ball by Ernie in the fifth minute and a sustained defensive effort in the second half earned Town a point in a 1-1 draw at Reading. When Dave Meeson, Reading's 'keeper was penalized for carrying the ball outside the penalty area, Town were awarded an early free-kick. In a beautifully executed manoeuvre Bobby Woodruff ran over the ball and Ernie lifted a sublime chip over Meeson's despairing dive into the back of the net off the crossbar. In a match that marked Roger Smart's League debut, Reading restored equilibrium in the twenty-fifth minute through Dennis Allen.

In April 1962 Ernie was honoured to play in Maurice Owen's testimonial match against an All-Stars XI. Ernie gave Swindon the lead following a neat one-two between Arnold Darcy and Bobby Woodruff. Ernie received the ball on the edge of the penalty area and hammered it past Lawrie Leslie off the underside of the bar. The All-Stars recovered to secure victory 5-4 in a highly entertaining and emotional evening. Scorers for the All-Stars side, which also included Billy Wright, Tom Finney and Roger Hunt, were Terry Paine and two each from David Layne and Peter McParland. Darcy, Jack Smith and Bill Atkins were the other Swindon scorers.

When I got into the team and played with Maurice, it was like a dream, can you imagine playing with your idol? He was a lovely man and looked after me when I came into the side. I had a lot of honours in the game, but to play with Maurice was my schoolboy dream and nothing ever eclipsed it. I can honestly say it was the highlight of my career.

In July 2000 Owen died at the age of seventy-six after suffering a stroke. He ranked alongside Harold Fleming, Harry Morris and Don Rogers as one of the greatest players to star for Swindon. He was a one-club man, declining a host of offers to leave for more glamorous and lucrative pastures, and retired at the end of the 1962/63 campaign after 591 League appearances for the Robins. He scored 148 League goals and won an England 'B' cap, but many observers felt he would have played for the full international side if he had plied his trade at a bigger club. Owen's death tugged many a heartstring.

I met a fellow called Geoff Price, who was a great Swindon fan down at the cattle market. He remembered every aspect of my game – one day he asked me, 'Do you remember that goal you scored with your right foot from the edge of the penalty area in the fifth minute on your comeback game after you broke your foot?' Incredible! Geoff told me Maurice had died and took me to the funeral, as I was banned from driving at the time. I didn't know Maurice had been unwell, so it was a hell of a shock when I heard the news. I cried my eyes out at the funeral, it was so sad and like the end of an era.

Swindon were not yet a great side, but inexorable progress had been made. The statisticians rushed to offer proof – they lost only four of their last twenty-five

1962 – Ernie's hero Maurice Owen (centre) with England stars Tom Finney and Billy Wright before Owen's testimonial match.

matches to reach the dizzy heights of ninth in the Third Division. The highlight was when Halifax were impaled 6-0, another two goals from Ernie (the others from Darcy, also with two, Woodruff and Smith), confirming him as top-scorer with 18 goals from 41 League appearances. Confidence was at an all-time high, particularly as Ernie and Mike Summerbee acknowledged they often met stiffer opposition in the summer as grave-diggers!

When I was sixteen I went to a cemetery in Radnor Street, near to where I lived in Swindon, and got talking to this old fella. He told me he earned ten shillings to dig up a grave, they called them 're-openers,' where other members of the family wanted to be buried with their loved ones. I put my name forward with Mike and we got the job during the summer before we turned professional. In the evening instead of looking at the sports pages, we'd look at the 'Deaths' column and say, "Look we've got £3 coming in this week!" We'd work overtime some weeks and rake in about fifteen quid, which was much more than I was getting playing for Swindon as an apprentice! There was another fella working there, who was really eerie. Soon after we first started we sat down to have a cup of tea in the mortuary and heard this voice. We thought it was the dead talking to us, but this fella would be walking about talking to himself, but we didn't see him! Sometimes our spade would go straight through a coffin. Mike would be really worried about this as he was more serious than I was in those days. I would say, 'Leave it, he's dead anyway!' I would sometimes get a small shovel of dirt and throw it on top of him – he didn't always share my sense of humour.

I also worked on the council one summer with Bill Atkins. We cut the grass verges and the grass in Westcott Park and also did a bit of planting and cleaned the toilets. We both got the sack as one lunchtime we'd had a few drinks at the Cock Robin and were due to cut a garden with this enormous mower. I thought I could get it through this gap to the garden, but the mower got stuck on the accelerator, went through three gardens and knocked several fences down! Next to the Cock Robin was the Ring coffee bar run by Gerry Williams, who became a lifelong friend. We also cleaned the toilets and rationed the toilet paper. We were told not to give the punters more than three pieces of paper and explained, 'No, sorry, it's down to the council.'

Another summer I did a spot of painting and decorating with Arnold Darcy and Peter Chamberlain. One day we were doing up a roof. I knew Arnold hated the sight of blood, so I told Peter I was going round the back of the house and pretend to fall off the ladder. I told him to leave it five minutes while I plastered myself with tomato sauce, then let out this bloodcurdling scream. Peter shouted, 'That sounds like Ernie,' and let Arnie come round the back first. He went white as a sheet when he saw me, especially as he was employing me and was probably worried about the insurance as well. I was reasonable at painting, apart from the fact that I was colour-blind, which was a bit of a handicap! Mike Summerbee and I went to the SAS camp by mistake to do a painting job once. We had to go into a big office to explain ourselves and realized we'd gone to the wrong Army camp in Herefordshire!

Other players had summer occupations: Bill Atkinson was also a lorry driver, Keith Morgan and Keith Colsell worked in a cigarette factory, Bobby Woodruff was a builder, Cliff Jackson a plasterer, Willie Harber was a hardware salesman and Terry Wollen worked in his father's off-licence. Ernie was also employed in an unusual supplementary trade for a footballer.

My dad cut all his mates' hair in the factory at BR to make his money up – he also cut mine. When I was thirteen I also started cutting hair and practised on my mates. When I was playing for Swindon I opened a hairdressing shop in the town with a mate called John Piff. I had been learning off my dad and cutting boys' hair at school. John cut my hair and I thought I could do as well as he could, and we agreed to go halves. Before we opened the shop, John was working for another gentleman in the town. I offered to cut Mike Summerbee's hair in the shop one day to get more practise in. I had cut it before but in our house. I tried to cut round his ear, but unfortunately nipped the top part of it. There was blood spurting all over the place and I'm sure the people waiting in the shop must have been praying I wasn't going to cut their hair next!

It cost next to nothing to pay for the rent etc, so I would train in the morning and cut hair in the afternoon. There was a brothel just over the other side of the park and the girls used to come to me for their condoms. I used to make more money out of them than the haircuts! I gave my half-interest away to John when I went to Wolves and carried on practising cutting hair at Jim and Sid's shop in Wolverhampton. My own favourite hairstyle, when I had some hair, was a D.A., a duck's arse, it waved at the back.

Four
Promotion Beckons and an England Call: 1962-1963

Bert Head was an early advocate of removing his squad for pre-season training. Prior to the commencement of the 1962/63 season the players decamped to Weymouth, staying at the Seaview Holiday Camp. The day's schedule would not necessarily be approved by a contemporary sports dietician, starting with pre-breakfast PT followed by a traditional fry-up of bacon and eggs. They then sweated their way through two and a half hours of ball practice in the blazing summer sunshine.

We'd go to the camp and stay in a massive tent for two weeks. Bert would say to us, 'Bob, Mick and Ern, get the cooking tent up.' We developed a great team spirit and I felt fitter than at any time in my career. I'm sure it played a big part of our success that season.

From set piece or open play, Town were in irresistible form from the outset and in September 1962 humiliated a woeful Brighton side 5-1, as Ernie bagged a brilliant hat-trick. Town opened the scoring after twelve minutes, when Keith Morgan surged down the right and snapped across a centre to Cliff Jackson, who headed in from close range. Ernie added a second six minutes later when Jackson took a free-kick that reached Jack Smith. Smith turned and pushed it back to the lively Ernie, who brought it down and coolly converted. Following a corner from Arnold Darcy, Jackson and Ernie challenged for the ball in the goalmouth. From a jumble of bodies, Smith jumped to nod it home and give Town a 3-0 lead at half-time. Ernie's second goal came within a minute of the restart. Collecting a ball on the right from Darcy, he ran unchallenged deep into enemy territory and let fly from fifteen yards. The ball raced inside the near post past the helpless Bert McGonigal, who reacted as if expecting a cross. McGonigal was relieved later when his goal survived another fine, fast-flowing move, culminating in Ernie hitting the bar. He then had to tip Ernie's curling free-kick over the bar. Ernie had not finished torturing the opposition defence, as he completed his hat-trick with a penalty after being fouled inside the box

Swindon Town 1962/63. From left to right, back row: Morgan, Woodruff, Owen, Wollen, Trollope. Front row: Summerbee, Hunt, Smith, Atkins, Jackson.

by Steve Burtenshaw. Mike Turner in the Swindon goal had only two serious shots to trouble him throughout, one being a penalty converted by Roy Jennings after Terry Wollen had brought down Peter Donnelly. Six points from four games and Swindon were flying – Ernie was described as 'conspicuous with his sniping.'

Turner; Wollen, Trollope; Morgan, Owen, Woodruff; Darcy, Hunt, Smith, Smart, Jackson.

I used to be a bit superstitious. My first hat-trick in senior football against Brighton was in a night game and on the afternoon of the match I went mushrooming with my dad in the fields nearby. When I scored the hat-trick I thought I'd have to do that for the next match and of course we didn't score a goal for the next two games. A couple of other superstitions were I was always last but one to run out onto the pitch and used to share my chewing gum with Donald Rogers.

Town sustained their promising form with a 3-0 victory over Wrexham later the same month. In the thirty-seventh minute Roger Smart put Swindon ahead with a delicately placed header, which Kevin Keelan touched but only succeeded in helping into the net. In the fifty-second minute Fox sent Jack Smith sprawling just outside the penalty area and to the left of the goal. From the resultant free-kick Ernie, swift of mind, spotted a gap in the wall and steered a low drive into the corner of the net, a foot beyond the reach of the diving Keelan. Ernie always had a reputation as a deadly penalty kicker, but by this stage of his career had also developed a reputation for an equally effective technique with free-kicks within sight of goal. Sometimes he preferred the delicate lob, but typically he allied punch with precision as in this case. Six minutes from time Smith crossed from the right and, as Keelan attempted to flick the ball away, Ernie nipped just in front of him to head home. The victory extended the Robins' undefeated run to seven games.

Ernie had also perfected the near-post headed flick-on from Bobby Woodruff, a pioneer of the long throw, which caused confusion in opposition penalty areas. With his stocky frame, another great attribute was his ability to hold the ball up, to shield it before bringing his teammates into the game. His all-round game continued to flourish and it was no surprise to see clubs continue to make advances in Bert Head's direction. In October 1962 Swindon turned down a bid of £30,000 from Plymouth Argyle. Argyle manager Ellis Stuttard, who had been on the training staff at Swindon, was quoted at the time as saying, 'Ernie is not just a very good footballer, he is one of the finest inside-forwards in any division of the League.' The directors passed a unanimous decision to reject the bid, having never previously been tempted by a cheque of £20,000 plus. They had effectively passed a vote of confidence in the promotion prospects of Head's young side, although the inclement weather caused a temporary blip in their aspirations.

During the Big Freeze we played QPR at home (January 1963). When we got to the ground Bert sent Harry Cousins into town with a couple of the lads who weren't playing with all our foot measurements. He came back with a dozen pairs of Bata boots for us to wear, like basketball boots, with thick rubber soles. They cost 12s 11d a pair, 65p in modern coinage. We beat them 5-0 and the headlines said, 'Bert's Babes' Bata Boots.'

An away fixture at Hull was not so successful when abandoned at half-time with the score goalless. Wind stopped play, whipping the loose snow off the pitch and in forty-five minutes turning it into an ice-rink. Swindon, nippier and safer in their basketball boots, gave the Hull defence a roasting in the early stages, but couldn't get the 'puck' into the back of the net. Town opened their FA Cup campaign with a first-round 4-2 victory over Reading. Despite being far from fully fit, Ernie received all the plaudits in the *Evening Advertiser* for an outstanding display: 'The lower divisions of the Football League occasionally produce a youngster of obvious international class, Johnny Byrne was one. Ernie Hunt, Swindon's inside right, is another. Throughout this tie Hunt was strapped from shoulder to thigh to ease the pain of a strained groin. Yet by the end even the most fervent Reading fans were applauding him. Hunt helped to break the deadlock in making the first goal and showed great judgement in scoring the second and fourth. The first goal disproved the theory that Swindon's long throw-in has become too well known to be effective. Reading fell for the Woodruff-Hunt speciality the first time it was tried. As the left half's throw from close to the corner flag dipped towards the near post, 'keeper Arthur Wilkie left his line and Hunt, in his well-rehearsed role, lifted the ball across for Jack Smith to nod over the goalkeeper's head. Two goals in two minutes set Swindon buzzing. At fifty-eight minutes Darcy started a move which ended in Hunt scoring with a beautiful glided header into the far side of the goal from Smith's cross. Almost from the restart an own goal by Dick Spiers from Jack Smith's drive increased the lead. Reading retaliated with a Walker penalty and a goal by Wheeler. In between Hunt met a Darcy cross with a perfect first-time running volley – sharp, low and at a deadly angle – that nearly uprooted the stanchion. Hunt stamped his personality over a gripping game.'

Following a relatively straightforward 2-0 away victory at Southern League Yeovil, where Ernie scored the opening goal and Cliff Jackson sealed the win, in the third round Town descended on Second Division Luton Town in supremely assured form. The match, delayed because of the weather, was just two days away from a potentially lucrative home tie against Everton. The Robins were sufficiently confident to have already printed 5,500 tickets for the Everton clash and swept into a 2-0 lead, Cliff Jackson scoring both goals in his basketball boots. The Town youngsters ran themselves into the ground to protect the lead and secured a notable victory. In reaching round four the boys, who cost a total of £4,100, were endeavouring to ambush an Everton side assembled by Harry Catterick with the support of Littlewoods chairman John Moores for £350,000. Hope dared to venture into Town hearts, but it was no surprise to see them exit 5-1 to the reigning League champions, with goals from Vernon (two), Gabriel, Morrissey and Bingham. Town's consolation was scored by Jack Smith. Ernie pitted his skills against Everton's new signing Tony Kay, at £55,000 the most expensive half-back in the world. Ernie, of course, cost Swindon a mere £10 signing-on fee.

Tony Kay marked me, it was his first game for Everton. He used to swagger, but I remember as he came out onto the pitch he slipped on his arse and fell over! Having said that, they were a good side and we were no match for them. I also remember my Auntie Ollie stood in the goalmouth before the game and pulled her big white drawers up, which revealed red-and-white-striped underwear! She would always do her party piece before the FA Cup matches.

Ernie's most prolific season thus far was a microcosm of Swindon's form, as they headed the League. He maintained his early promise with further braces in a 3-3 draw at Watford in February and a 2-1 victory against Reading in March, where he was at full throttle, torturing the opposition in their own backyard. Nerves seeped into Town's play however, when they suffered a setback at Easter with a 3-2 defeat at home to Colchester, despite both goals again coming from Ernie. The Robins promptly managed to regroup and the following day thrashed Colchester 6-1 at the County Ground, Ernie once again obliging twice. John Stevens notched a hat-trick, his first goal coming immediately before the interval, and added the other two in the first five minutes of the second half, completing his hat-trick in six minutes of playing time. The pick of his goals was the second when, after an elegant move contrived by Keith Morgan and Mike Summerbee, he powerfully beat two defenders before unleashing a crisp shot, which beat the despairing dive of Percy Ames. Summerbee had opened the scoring after eight minutes and Ernie's first came in the sixty-sixth. Stevens threaded a ball through to Ernie, whose initial shot was parried by Ames, but he had plenty of time to compose himself and knock in the rebound. Ernie completed the rout five minutes from time when ghosting through the scrambled defence. Colchester's sole response came from King in the eighteenth minute, and the match also marked the League debut of eighteen-year-old Willie Harber, deputizing for the injured Bobby Woodruff.

Town were on a high and in May 1963, after forty-two long years in the wilderness, promotion was clinched in the last home game of the season against Shrewsbury. The visitors spent most of the match attacking an over-anxious Swindon side with some entertaining football, but lacked a killer touch in front of goal. It was fortunate for the Robins that Shrewsbury player-manager Arthur Rowley had rested himself, otherwise the result may have been different. On a muddy, slippery pitch, the only time Swindon looked like dominating was midway through the first half, when they found visiting 'keeper Miller in good form. Following a sliced defensive clearance, he rushed out of goal to deny Ernie as he raced in, then threw himself to the left to push a loose ball away from Mike Summerbee. Ernie did find the back of the net just before half-time, but was given offside. Mike Turner was by far the busier 'keeper and had to throw himself at the feet of Middleton, as the inside right bore in on goal. Swindon nearly went behind midway through the second half, but for a desperate goal-line clearance from Owen Dawson. As Gregson broke through on the right-hand side, Turner stuck out a foot to intercept the winger's close-range drive, but the ball rebounded to Clarke. The centre forward lobbed it towards the empty goal, but somehow Dawson managed to head the ball out from under the bar. Perhaps Swindon knew it would be their night as Roger Smart, with just a handful of appearances to his name, scored the only goal two minutes from time. John Stevens challenged Miller on the edge of the penalty area and the ball ran loose to Smart out on the left wing. Smart hit it towards goal as Miller backtracked and, although the 'keeper got his hands to the ball, he could not keep it out. Swindon fans, dressed to the nines, filled the air with songs and chants as the drama unfurled. When all was settled, the bubbly freely mixed with perspiration in the dressing room.

Alongside the donkey free-kick game, the most memorable match I played in was when we beat Shrewsbury and got promoted to the Second Division for the first time. Roger scored the only goal in the eighty-eighth minute in front of over 20,000. It was an evening game, which always generated a different atmosphere in my career. It was great to get one over Shrewsbury, as they had been our bogey team in the past and it was another tight game. Our captain Keith Morgan was an inspiration – he played out of his skin and snuffed out their forward line. Most of the supporters came onto the pitch at the end and by the time we got back to the dressing room I only had my jock-strap on – it was the same for all the players.

Turner; Dawson, Trollope; Morgan, McPherson, Woodruff; Summerbee, Hunt, Stevens, Smart, Jackson.

We played one more game that season, away at Hull City. Midway through the first half Bobby Woodruff took one of his long throws towards me at the near post. I held this guy, caught it on my chest, swung round and volleyed it in from about six yards with such force that it went through the side netting. I automatically turned round and put my hand up, as I initially thought it went into the net legitimately. As we ran back to the centre spot, the full-back who I had held off ran up to me and said he was going to get me. Later in the game when we had a corner, before the ball came over he lifted me up, head-butted me twice and gave me two black eyes. The referee didn't see a thing.

The Robins finished the season runners-up to Northampton Town, using a system of fast and simple football. Ernie's contribution was 24 goals from 43 League games, no less than twelve of them following long throws by Bobby Woodruff. Two ever-presents in the victorious side were captain Keith Morgan and John Trollope.

Ernie's performances in the cup against higher-class opposition enabled him to gain the international recognition that eluded him at schoolboy level, when he was selected for the England Under-23 team on 2 June 1963. England were beaten by the odd goal in an ill-tempered match against Romania, but deserved a draw after applying heavy pressure for sustained periods in the second half. In a strong wind on a heavy pitch, England were dominant for the first quarter of an hour, with Ernie foraging up front in the unaccustomed position of centre forward. Colin Dobson, who also made his debut, was desperately unlucky not to score after fifteen minutes with an acrobatic overhead kick which rocked the crossbar. Romania hardly had a worthwhile shot on goal, but scored after thirty-four minutes from a soft free-kick by Matei on the edge of the penalty area that dipped over the wall. It was a tough debut for Ernie, who was man-marked for much of the game by Petescu. After Derek Stokes had replaced Freddie Hill in the fortieth minute, Ernie moved to inside right, where he used the ball intelligently. He grew in maturity as the game progressed and was unlucky not to grab an equalizer twenty minutes from time. Ernie stabbed out his right foot to a cross from Ian Callaghan, but his shot was parried by the 'keeper Suciu. According to the *Evening Advertiser* Ernie 'made an impressive debut... showing the poise and cultured approach so familiar to Swindon supporters, with a display which confirmed his high potential in top-class football.' England manager Joe Mercer was reported as saying he felt Ernie was the best forward on show that day. Bobby Thomson was generally felt England's most impressive performer, cutting out the threat of Romania's number-one forward, Matei, while Alan Hinton and Graham Cross also had fine matches.

Bonetti; Cohen, Thomson; Cross, Labone, Deakin; Callaghan, Hill (Stokes), Hunt, Dobson, Hinton.

We had a good side at Swindon in those days and our forward line really clicked when we were promoted, which helped me win my first international cap when I was twenty. Bobby Tambling couldn't go on tour to Romania with the Under-23s, so they got in touch with Bert. He didn't know where I was and found me out of town painting with Arnold Darcy and Peter Chamberlain. Bert drove up in his car and said, 'You'd better get going, they want you to fly out to Romania tomorrow.' I went straight home, packed my bag, drove to London, got a passport and visa and flew out to Bucharest in a matter of hours.

TELEGRAMA
ECHIPA DE FOOTBAL ENGLEZA *LA Hotel LIDO*
ERNIE HUNT CHEZ ENGLAND FOOTBALL

Primitor   **PARTY BUKAREST**

Nr
BUC1206 1168 SWINDON 20 1 1223   data   ora   m

CONGRATULATIONS AND BEST WISHES FOR TODAYS GAME
FROM ALL AT THE COUNTY GROUND

M.T.Tc. 8-01 (Ktg. 6-20) 1/12 A 1

June 1963 – Ernie received a telegram in Bucharest from the County Ground on making his England Under-23 debut.

Playing in Romania when I was still at Swindon was not easy, especially as the other lads, like Ian Callaghan, who was my roommate, were regulars for First Division sides. It was a big step, but I seemed to take it in my stride. I wore the number nine shirt and wanted to keep the jersey, although it wasn't the done thing in those days. However me being me, I gave it away to the son of Harold Smith, who was my business partner in the sports shop I later had in Coventry.

Later on Alf Ramsey watched me play one game where I knew I was feeling below par. There was an Under-23 game coming up at Bristol City and I expected to be playing in place of Bobby Tambling, who was injured, but I was made reserve and Geoff Hurst played. As it was so close to Swindon, it disappointed thousands of our supporters, so when I got there I asked him why I wasn't in the team. Alf told me that the last time he saw me he thought I was struggling and playing very deep. I said I could hardly breathe as I had tonsillitis. He explained I shouldn't have been playing if I had been ill, but I just wanted to play all the time in those days and I think that cost me a full cap.

Five
The Robins Crash-Land
1963-1965

The town was buzzing with unprecedented expectancy during the summer of 1963 and the Robins honed their pre-season training at an international tournament in Belgium. In the opening game Swindon defeated Austria Innsbruck 2-0.

I scored both goals then this bloke started man-marking me. I went down to the corner flag and he followed me. He was kicking me all over the park and in the end I smacked him in the face and got sent off. I was so disappointed I missed the final and perhaps I learnt a lesson from that as, apart from when Wolves played in America, I only got sent off one other time in my career.

Swindon cruised through to the final, where they trounced Sporting Zebras from Charleroi 8-1, Keith Colsell deputizing for the suspended Ernie.

Ernie marked Swindon's historic first match in the Second Division against Scunthorpe in August 1963 with the opening goal sixteen minutes into the game. It was a header from close range – despite his lack of inches he was always good in the air – and was netted at the Stratton Bank end. As Town inexorably built up the pressure he scored a second in the 3-0 victory (the other coming from John Stevens), and netted again in the next fixture at Grimsby (2-1) before missing two matches with tonsillitis. Astonishingly Town won their first six fixtures of the season, culminating in a 3-0 defeat of Manchester City on a mild September night in front of a record League crowd of 28,173 shoe-horned into the County Ground. Despite feeling below par, Ernie was in the thick of things, asserting himself and helping to write the words for a famous victory. He scored the third, following goals from Mike Summerbee and Jack Smith.

I was suffering so much right from the start of the 1963/64 season with tonsillitis that the club made an appointment for me to see a specialist in Cirencester. I was twenty and the specialist said I would have to have my tonsils out. At that

Swindon Town 1963/64. From left to right, back row: McPherson, Wollen, Atkins, Turner, Harvey, Morgan, Lloyd. Second row; Plumb, Trollope, Hallett, French, Hicks, Smith, Smart, Dawson, Summerbee. Third row; Thorburn, Shergold, Griffin, Rogers, Hellin, Stevens, Leggett, Huxford, Woodruff, Sproats, Peapell. Fourth row: Lewis, Tabor, Harber, Darcy, Cousins (Trainer), Head (Manager), Morse (Secretary), Colsell, Hunt, Ling, James. Front row: Critchley, Leroy Hedges, W. Corbett, Wrintmore, Leslie Hedges.

age it was a bigger operation as you generally had them out as a kid, so I was not particularly looking forward to it. The club thought they'd given me enough time to get back from the specialist for the game with Manchester City. I drove back but there was so much traffic I got to the ground late. The gateman was fairly new and didn't recognize me. 'I'm Ernie Hunt' I pleaded with him. 'That's a good 'un,' he said and in the end he had to be persuaded by the supporters to let me in. I had my tonsils out later in the season, when I missed the West Ham FA Cup tie. I was in hospital and could hardly breathe by then.

In October 1963 John Boorman wrote and directed a TV programme about the club called *Six Days to Saturday*. It was repeated in 2003, having been rediscovered in the BBC vaults. Condensed into just over half an hour, it provided a unique insight into a week in the life of Swindon Town and the lifestyle of the players. Thirty-year-old Boorman, of course, became one of Britain's most distinguished film makers. Much of the footage is 'priceless.' 'We get wild pigeons nest in the roof of the stand and they make a hell of a mess,' says a local, taking pot-shots at the birds. He passes his shotgun to Bobby Woodruff, who takes aim himself. Ernie is filmed cutting Bert Head's hair. 'I can't do a Beatles cut yet,' says Ernie, so Bert settles for a 'Yul Brynner.' 'I've got blood on the scissors', remarks Ernie. 'Blood on them wing-halves, never mind them scissors,' replies Bert. The narrative reflects an altogether different era: 'They indulge in mindless pursuits in the afternoon like driving aimlessly in the country, but professional footballers can't afford to be too interested in the world, their career makes ruthless demands on mind as well as body. They are known and watched, so must conform to public notions of virtue. Ernie and Mike Summerbee derive comfort from this (Redcliffe) street of cosy back-to-backs,' as they play football with the kids in the street. Mike buys a bag of sweets in the local shop for sevenpence, while seventeen-year-old Don Rogers has breakfast in bed at the club hostel on the morning of the match. Ernie and Mike drive to the match in Ernie's car, an Austin A35. 'On a Saturday morning the people of the street watch, but leave them alone. Ernie Hunt is the favourite, his picture is pinned under the desk-lid of many a Swindon schoolgirl.'

The film features superb coverage of the home game against Leyton Orient, with a shot of Don Rogers beating three men in the first half before chipping the ball from the byeline into the box. The ball is partially deflected by a defender and Ernie instinctively volleys the ball past Davies before anyone else can react for the first goal. After seven games without scoring, normal service is resumed for Ernie as he clasps his hands over his head in delight. Despite taking a slender lead, at half-time Bert Head delivers his team talk: 'Now we're not going well at all, you know that as well as I do, our passing is a little astray.' The players respond to Head's demands and put on a virtuoso performance in the second half, with four goals in a devastating fourteen-minute spell. Mike Summerbee increases the lead with a volley, followed by a low angled drive from Rogers for the third. Keith Morgan evades two tackles to make it four after fifty-five minutes with a shot inside the far post. Four minutes from the end Jack Smith sends in a deft cross from the left and Ernie strokes in the fifth from close range. Star turn is seventeen-year-old Don Rogers, with early notice of the silky runs he would grace at the highest level in a performance that gives the Leyton Orient defenders a torrid afternoon. The film ends with the players trooping out of the ground after the match, bearing satisfying smiles following their endeavours.

When I looked at the faces on the Stratton Bank end, I felt I recognized so many of the crowd on the terraces, it was very emotional for me to see the video again, it was unbelievable. You can just see my Mum and Dad in Redcliffe Street looking out of our house when I was kicking the ball about with the kids. I used to make sure all the Swindon lads were around when I cut Bert's hair and would say to him, 'Same price, half a crown, but you will pick me this week, won't you boss?'

Despite being dogged by illness, Ernie was determined to play in the following week's match at Plymouth. Town came from behind twice to equalize before gaining a strong grip in the second half, with two well-taken goals in the last six minutes. Former Swindon favourite Cliff Jackson opened the scoring for Plymouth after fifteen minutes, only for Ernie to equalize four minutes later from an indirect free-kick. His shot rebounded off the wall, but before anyone could react Ernie slammed in the rebound high into the net. O'Neill restored Plymouth's lead four minutes from the interval and Swindon responded by pushing Ernie forward at the beginning of the second half. Jack Smith played a deeper role and the switch paid dividends in the sixty-second minute with Ernie's second after Leiper was only able to palm a left-wing cross out towards the edge of the penalty area. Ernie was there to return the ball sharply into an unguarded net. Don Rogers headed Town into the lead and the victory was sealed by a stunning thirty-five-yard free-kick from Bobby Woodruff, his first of the season. Swindon had played with great purpose and determination and overall were excellent value for the victory.

In the FA Cup, Town beat Aldershot in round four before going out to West Ham in front of another record crowd in excess of 28,000. Ernie was denied the opportunity of pitting his wits against Bobby Moore's men, by virtue of having his tonsils out.

Tactics time with manager Bert Head. From left, clockwise: Summerbee, Hunt, Stevens, Atkins, Head, Smith, Trollope, Turner, Woodruff, Hallett, Smart, Morgan, Dawson, Rogers.

A relaxed group of Swindon players during training. From left to right, back row: Woodruff, Smart, Trollope, Hallett, Hunt, Summerbee, Rogers. Front row: Turner, Stevens, Dawson, Morgan, McPherson, Atkins, Smith.

Bert was a funny bloke – when we played West Ham it was a big match, so we went away to train in secret for a few days. He didn't want us to tell anyone where we were going. However the cameras went to film us training and Bert was interviewed right in front of the pier at Weston-super-Mare! We were having a bit of a dip in form in the League round about that time when Bert asked Mike Summerbee and I out to judge a Miss Wroughton competition. It was a Friday night and we were surprised when Bert offered us a pint, especially after he bought us a second one during the evening. We lost 2-1 to Huddersfield the next day (April 1964) and Bert called everyone in for a team meeting on the Monday. 'You're not concentrating,' he said, 'not doing this and that, and I even had two players out drinking on a Friday night!' That was typical Bert.

Following Cliff Jackson's transfer to Plymouth, March 1964 saw the second of Head's talented youngsters, Bobby Woodruff, depart, when he moved to Wolves for £35,000. Although Ernie felt less than 100 per cent fit several times during the campaign, he top-scored for the fourth consecutive season with 12 goals in 34 League appearances, as the team finished in a respectable fourteenth place.

The 1964/65 season saw Swindon struggle in the League and major factors were a series of misfortunes which befell Ernie, who was appointed captain during the campaign. In September he had a benefit match at the County Ground when Town again hosted Manchester City. A crowd of 17,135, over 10,000 down on the corresponding fixture the previous season, endured a miserable 1-0 defeat for the home side.

For my benefit match I made £145. They went round with a big sheet and the crowd threw coins into it. I didn't keep the gate receipts or anything. Even though it was a difficult season, it was a great honour for me to be made captain of my home town team. We were going through a bad spell in the League and Bert held a team meeting to clear the air and talk about what was going wrong. I found myself saying more than most players, which ones among us weren't taking responsibility. I didn't exclude myself, as I wasn't scoring enough goals. After the meeting Bert relieved Keith Morgan of his duties, which he was very upset about, and made me captain.

There was still plenty of humour around the club. Bert called me in one day to say we'd signed Frank Haffey. When I reminded him that Frank was Scotland's goalkeeper when they lost 9-3 to England in 1961, Bert said, 'But Ernie, he does a brilliant Al Jolson, which will be great for the Christmas party!' It was raining heavily the day before a home game, with the lime for the pitch, which was normally machine spread, going all over the place. In the end Bert got hold of a load of lime in his hands, but every time he put it down the wind blew it in all directions. He just wanted the match to go ahead, he was so enthusiastic about the game.

One bright spot was a 4-2 home defeat of Derby County at the beginning of October, when Ernie distinguished himself with the second hat-trick of his senior career. The visitors went ahead with a goal from Eddie Thomas in the seventeenth minute. Town responded within three minutes when Ernie converted a penalty awarded for handball. That proved the spur for relentless pressure and five minutes from the interval Ernie scrambled in the second. On the stroke of half-time Owen Dawson added a third. Early in the second half Ernie completed his hat-trick with a smart header past Reg Matthews. Ernie's goals were enough in themselves to establish him as Man of the Match, but he also merited that distinction on the strength of his brilliant midfield work, which was witnessed by two representatives of Wolves. He was not able to demonstrate his consistency of the previous season because of recurring bouts of tonsillitis, but was right back to his most cultured and scintillating form. An

England Under-23 selector was at the match, which raised hopes that Ernie would be able to add to his single cap. Bert Head enthused, 'I thought he was unlucky to get only one game. Ernie was watched two or three times by the selectors last season, but unfortunately his form was affected by his bouts of tonsillitis which, I am sure cost him a cap. We have recommended him again and on his present form, I think he must have a fine chance.'

Following a 3-3 home draw with Cardiff on 17 October, Ernie's early season form was again interrupted when he was admitted to hospital for an appendicitis operation.

I was driving to Abingdon in the evening to have a few drinks with Maurice Owen and my stomach was aching so much, they rushed me into hospital to have my appendix out. When I had tonsillitis I think it went down my body. On the Sunday morning when I woke up, the local choir were going round the wards singing – I thought I was in heaven! Bert Head also came to see me on the Sunday and said, 'Ernie, how long will it be before you can play?' I was back within two months.

Years later when I had my first hip operation, a lad in the ambulance asked if his father could come and see me in hospital. When I came round after the anaesthetic the first face I saw was an old boy with a dog collar right in front of my face. I didn't realize this lad's father was a vicar and I really thought I was in trouble that time!

When Ernie returned in December 1964, Town had plummeted uncomfortably close to the bottom of the League. A series of indifferent results preceded a personal disaster for Ernie on 23 March 1965 when, despite notching two goals in a 4-2 victory over Northampton Town, he chipped a bone in his foot which again sidelined him. When the plaster was taken off on 14 April the relegation situation was dire and Ernie was rushed back to action within three days, although palpably unfit. It looked to be a masterstroke when Town recorded a 3-2 win over Rotherham but, after superbly cracking in Swindon's first goal within five minutes, triumph turned to disaster when he limped off in the second half, his foot clearly distressed, and he missed the remainder of the season.

I had a good game against Northampton – they were top of the League and we were struggling– but I got injured when I kicked the bottom of Frank Large's boot, which is not something I would recommend to anyone. Mike Summerbee also took a knock so the morning after, when he picked me up from my girlfriend's, we both went to hospital. He had an x-ray and was ok, but I had two broken bones in my right foot and thought that was me out for *the rest of the season. They put a plaster up to my knee and told me to come back in six weeks time to take it off. I wondered what the hell Bert was going to say. Mike walked first into Bert's small office, I went in behind and of course he couldn't see my leg. Bert said, 'Everything all right, Mike?' 'Yes fine.' Then he looked at me, 'Everything... what the **** is all that?' 'I've broken my foot in two places, boss.' He said, 'That's no good to me, we've got six games to play!'*

I sat in the dugout to watch the lads training and as the ball came across I instinctively kicked it with the inside of my foot. I couldn't feel anything and Bert saw me and said to Harry Cousins, 'Get hold of him and put him in the boot room.' He cut the top of my plaster off, so all he left was where it covered my foot. 'Who's got the biggest boots in here?' They belonged to Vincent Jack, who played centre half for the reserves, he was 6ft 5in and had size twelve boots. He cut the toe-cap in half, opened all the laces out and fitted my foot in plaster! 'Go and put your training gear on,' said Bert. All the lads cheered as I came out. 'Have a run on the side,' said Bert. I started limping and Bert put his hand on his head in despair. 'No good Harry, get him changed and take him to hospital.' They took me to see Dr Louis, who was a highly respected surgeon in the West Country. Bert went to see him first, I think to try and persuade him I could play. Dr Louis said to me, 'Ernie, you can't do any more damage to your foot, as it's already broken!' So they rushed me back in less than a month. I scored on my return against Rotherham, but broke it again. I came off ten minutes from the end and they took me straight to hospital to put it back in plaster. Bert was so keen and enthusiastic, he talked me into playing many times when I shouldn't have. I always wanted to play so thought nothing of a cortisone injection to get me out on the pitch.

Another time I remember straining my groin the week before an important game. During the week they tied me with this strapping round my middle. Harry and Bert said, 'Put some across there and another there,' and then asked me how it felt. I did some jogging around and knew it didn't make any difference but said, 'That feels better,' as I didn't want to miss a game. On the match day they forgot which way they did the strapping up and all the lads were hysterical as Bert and Harry were rowing about how the strapping went on. It was a waste of time as I didn't play but I was soon back! What with my tonsillitis, my appendix out and my broken foot it was not surprising that there was a bit of a dip in my form from time to time.

Swindon had to make do without their star forward for six of the final seven games and failed to win any. The loss of such a key player at a crucial time was felt to be the difference between survival and relegation. Surprisingly the Football League allowed fellow relegation candidates Portsmouth to play on the evening of the last day of the season, after Town had lost 2-1 at Southampton. Knowing they only needed a point to stay up, Portsmouth drew 1-1 away to already promoted Northampton and Swindon were demoted to the Third Division. Ernie made 29 League appearances, scoring 11 goals, a highly respectable ratio in a struggling side. Bert Head claimed that, without illness and injury to the Town's 'best young player,' the club wouldn't have been relegated. Shortly after the end of the season, Head was deemed surplus to requirements and dismissed, despite guiding the Robins to the greatest day in the club's history to date. He was soon back in the game managing Bury and one of his finest hours was subsequently taking Crystal Palace into the First Division for the first time in 1968/69. On a personal front, Ernie was set to tie the knot with girlfriend Anne.

I met Anne in 1960 at Westcott Youth club in Swindon when she was about fifteen. I married her in 1965 at the end of the season, at St Augustine's in Swindon. Dave Webb was best man. We went on our stag night to our local just outside Swindon, the Spotted Cow. They took the plaster off my broken foot on the day of my stag night, which was the night before my wedding, just in time for me to hobble up the aisle. It was May Day, 1 May and it wasn't very good planning as it was also FA Cup final day. We went to the Station Hotel in Swindon for our reception and to Kensington for our honeymoon. I was moaning as I was missing the match, but as we walked into our hotel in London, I heard this cheering upstairs as the final went into extra time. I left Anne and dashed upstairs to watch Liverpool beat Leeds and she said, 'I know where you're going!'

Relegation saw the break-up of the exciting young team Head had constructed. Ernie played just five times back in the Third Division after requesting a transfer during the summer, having been seduced by the siren calls of clubs more elevated than Swindon. After Mike Summerbee was transferred in August 1965 to enjoy an illustrious career with Manchester City and England, Ernie moved to Second Division Wolves for £40,000 a month later. A record of 88 goals in 239 appearances made him Town's tenth-highest scorer of all time. His last game for Swindon was a low-key affair, a goalless draw at home to Walsall on 4 September, where he remained Town's most polished forward, but his efforts to bring more purpose into the line found little support. He was also injured, so failed to turn out three days later against Bristol Rovers.

The previous four seasons had contained the sharpest possible contrasts for Swindon. A steady rise to glory inspired, literally, by an intelligent youth policy, was followed by a year of disillusion made more poignant by the suddenness of the fall. Two seasons in the Second Division were all that were granted to Town after their long stay in the Third Division. In the process they lost the manager that had taken them up and perhaps some of the spirit that had got them there. Ernie paid tribute to some of his Robins' colleagues.

Roger Smart was a nice bloke who played up front and ran his socks off. He never got the recognition he deserved, as he used to do half my running, but then again I scored half his goals! Of the other lads, Keith Morgan was a strong player, a good man-marker and a nice bloke. He was really underestimated, but had trouble with his knees. Terry Wollen unluckily broke his leg against Notts County in 1962 and was never the same player again. John Trollope was 'Mr Reliable' and must have played about 14,000 games for Swindon. We played with two wingers, Mike Summerbee and Donald Rogers, who was very nervous to start with. Don didn't have to bother to come back, as Mike was up and down all the time.

I went to Molineux to watch Mike play for Manchester City against Wolves soon after he was transferred there. Cecil Green, who was friendly with Mike's dad and had a shop in the same street as us, asked me if I wanted to go. I sat next to Andy Beattie, but it had nothing to do with me going to Wolves shortly after. During the game Mike ran across Dave Woodfield, who barged him off the pitch. The stand in those days was right on the touchline and Mike split his head open on a metal post. I went into the dressing room to support him as they stitched him up. They put cotton wool over the top of it, he looked like he was covered in a snowstorm!

I knew quite a few clubs were interested in me and decided, if we went down, I would put in for a transfer, as I didn't want to play in the Third Division again and seven seasons was long enough to be with one club. Bert wouldn't let me go all the while we were in the Second Division, but that was fine by me as I didn't want to go anyway. I couldn't get going at Swindon back in the Third Division, it was difficult to keep my motivation in the end and was all very unsettling, although as ever I didn't want to let anybody down. I had no idea Wolves were interested in me, but Andy Beattie, who was known as the 'Flying Doctor' as he had spells as manager with so many clubs, signed me to play for them.

Incoming Swindon manager Danny Williams was reluctant to part with Ernie until a replacement was found, preferably in a player-exchange deal. Peter Knowles was initially offered to Swindon by Wolves in part-exchange, but declined the move. Aston Villa were also interested in Ernie, offering £25,000 plus winger Alan Baker in exchange, reflected in manager Dick Taylor's comments at the time, 'We've done everything possible to get Hunt and will continue our efforts. As regards a player-exchange, we will listen to any suggestions Swindon may make.' When Baker refused to move to a Third Division side, former Wolves star Barry Stobart was offered as an alternative. In the event Ernie eschewed the temptation to join Villa, who were languishing at the foot of the First Division and a straight cash deal was negotiated with Wolves. Ernie liked the set-up at Molineux and felt he would have more opportunity to show his ball-artist skills there.

The Wolves chairman John Ireland met me in Stratford to do a deal, then Danny Williams said Villa were also interested in me. I went to see what they had to say, but knew it wasn't for me, as I met Alan Baker and Dave Pountney while Danny spoke to Dick Taylor and they both said they weren't prepared to drop two divisions. I also didn't want to let Mr Ireland down, plus Bobby Woodruff had gone there, so I knew he would help me settle in.

Mr Ireland asked me how much I had been offered to go to Villa. I said '£3,000,' although I hadn't. He said, 'We'll give you £4,000,' which I was very happy with. Swindon didn't know anything about this, but John said he would phone me at nine the following morning. I hung around the dressing room and the others wondered why I wasn't getting changed for training when the phone went. Danny Williams the manager said, 'Ernie, come and speak to your new chairman.' I pretended I didn't know anything about it. Danny wanted me to get something for him for letting me go, which amazed me. I went to see Andy Beattie, who asked me what I wanted for my wages. I said, '£45 a week' and he replied, 'That will do.' Andy couldn't believe me when I told him about the lump sum I was being paid as a 'backhander' but it has always happened in football. Everyone knows about it, but I blew the money away as usual.

Roger Smart inherited the number eight shirt, but Danny Williams was active in the transfer market in an effort to search for a new formula to take Swindon back to the Second Division. He almost pulled off a major coup when asking Bury to name their price for Colin Bell. The deal fell through when Bert Head insisted on a player-exchange plus £35,000 – his distinguished career for Manchester City and England took off shortly after. Williams had no easy task in following Head, but he succeeded in bringing the League Cup to the County Ground in the memorable final of 1969, when Town heroically defeated Arsenal. Just Trollope, Morgan and Smart remained from the promotion-winning side of 1963, but Ernie's departure did allow Don Rogers' career to flourish, as it enabled him to assume greater responsibility in the side.

Six

As the Wolves Go Marching On
1965-1967

Until the end of the 1964/65 season, Wolverhampton Wanderers had enjoyed their longest spell in the First Division, stretching twenty-six seasons from 1932/33. During their halcyon days, they won the League championship in seasons 1953/54, 1957/58 and 1958/59. Andy Beattie was appointed caretaker-manager in November 1964 and used twenty-eight players in an unsuccessful attempt to keep the club in the top flight. Ernie was signed by Beattie on the morning of 17 September 1965, with every expectation of making his debut at Southampton the following day. But four hours after the signing was completed, Beattie resigned. Ernie decided he wasn't quite ready and watched from the stands as the Saints won 9-3. He did make his first start for the wounded Wolves in the following match, creating goals for Peter Knowles, Dave Wagstaffe and Terry Wharton in a 3-0 home win over Bury.

Andy said before the Southampton game, 'I can't play you tomorrow as I have already picked the team.' I said I didn't want to play anyway, as I would have taken Bobby Woodruff's place. Within hours Beattie had gone and our coach Ronnie Allen was looking after the team. I took my boots just in case and was quite pleased I didn't play in view of the result! I played in the next game against Bury, who were by then strangely managed by none other than Bert Head.

One of my main hopes was that Wolves would make me a deep-lying inside forward. I preferred that position, although I was happy to play anywhere on the park. I'd always been an inside forward, nearly always an inside right. The fans were pretty frustrated at the time. They'd seen their team sink into the Second Division after years of achievement in the First Division. The terraces were half-empty and a lot of the glamour had faded, although the atmosphere made me aware of the pride and history of a great club. Part of the reason for joining Wolves was that I was sure the good days would return to Molineux. We were part of the new era in the Wanderers' history.

When I first went there, I shared digs with John Holsgrove, who had just been transferred from Crystal Palace and made his debut with me in the Bury game. The landlady was a fresh-air fiend, there was ice on the windows when they were not wide open. It would not be unusual for me to come in and see John strumming his guitar with his overcoat on in bed!

After a promising initial period under the guidance of Ronnie Allen, Ernie's injury jinx struck again. The first ever Wolves substitute was Fred Goodwin, when he came on for Ernie against Middlesbrough at Molineux in October 1965.

I broke my right toe after scoring in the Middlesbrough game, but was only out for a fortnight, so just missed one game. I probably shouldn't have come back so quickly as the toe was still pretty painful but, as usual, I just wanted to play and the doctor gave me some painkillers. We went on an unbeaten run of ten games after I joined and just missed out on promotion. I was pleased with my start, as I managed to score 12 goals in 34 games.

Ronnie Allen was reshaping the side in readiness for the following season as Wolves finished in sixth place, and one of his most astute signings was Mike Bailey for £40,000 from Charlton Athletic in March 1966. Ernie's form had again been recognized at international level and he was rewarded with a further two appearances for the England Under-23 side during the season. His second international was against Yugoslavia at Southampton on 24 November 1965 when replacing Alan Ball, who played for the full international side a fortnight later. The 2-1 win was described as a competent victory over an experienced side containing seven internationals, three of whom had played against Norway in the World Cup two weeks earlier. Alex Stepney had three shots to face in ninety minutes – he saved the first and last, and had little chance with the goal in the seventieth minute, a low drive from Djajic following a rare breakaway. England took twenty-five minutes to find any rhythm, when George Armstrong played a short corner to local boy Martin Chivers, who eluded the opposition with a dribble along the byline. His low cross was deftly hooked in off the far post by Mick Jones for the first goal. Chivers himself scored the winner eleven minutes from the end with a well-judged header from a pinpoint Bobby Thomson cross. England overran the clever and experienced Yugoslavs for long periods, but many promising moves were nullified by the well-drilled defence. Tommy Smith was compared favourably with Nobby Stiles in defence and paired up well with Vic Mobley. John Hollins made a typically energetic impression and, in his Under-23 debut, Don Rogers gained in confidence as the game progressed. He linked well with Ernie, who worked hard and made several thoughtful passes, and also had a fierce drive from twenty-five yards

THE FOOTBALL ASSOCIATION

Patron: HER MAJESTY THE QUEEN
President: THE EARL OF HAREWOOD
Chairman: J. H. W. MEARS

Secretary:
DENIS FOLLOWS, M.B.E., B.A.

Telegraphic Address:
FOOTBALL ASSOCIATION, LONDON, W.2

22 LANCASTER GATE, LONDON, W.2

Ref: SLW/IMN

15th November, 1965

R. Hunt, Esq.,
c/o. Mr. J.T. Howley
Wolverhampton Wanderers Football Club,
Monileux Grounds,
Waterloo Road,
WOLVERHAMPTON

Dear Mr. Hunt,

INTERNATIONAL MATCH 'UNDER 23'
ENGLAND v. YUGOSLAVIA
SOUTHAMPTON - 24TH NOVEMBER 1965

I have pleasure in advising that you have been selected
to play   for England in the above Match at Southampton on
Wednesday, 24th November, 1965, kick-off 7.30 p.m.   Your Club has
already been informed of your selection.

An itinerary card is being prepared and will be sent to
you in due course, but, for your information, all Players will be
required to report at The Royal Hotel, Southampton, by 5.30 p.m.
on Monday, 22nd November, 1965.   There will be training and match
practice at Southampton on Monday evening and during the following
days.

The party travelling from London will assemble at
Waterloo Station opposite the departure platform at 3 p.m. for the
train leaving for Southampton at 3.30 p.m.   If you are travelling
via London you are invited to join the party.

Yours sincerely,

Secretary

November 1965 – a letter from the Football Association advising Ernie of his selection for the England
Under-23 side against Yugoslavia.

brilliantly turned over the bar by Pantelic. The *Daily Mirror* reported that, 'The industrious and impressive Hunt suggested he is a player with an international future... [he] was the springboard for many of England's first-half raids.'

Stepney; Lawler, Thomson; Hollins, Mobley, Smith; Armstrong, Hunt, Jones, Chivers, Rogers.

Ernie still has the general notes and instructions issued to him on joining the squad. 'In addition to travelling expenses, players taking part in the match will be paid a fee of £20. Shirts, shorts and stockings will be provided by the Football Association. Players are requested to bring with them athletic slips, shin guards and football boots, which must be properly studded. All players are advised to take with them soap and towels for personal use.' How times change.

I waited two and a half years for my second cap – I didn't feel I had lost my sparkle, but I was injured a lot of the time. It didn't affect my form too much, just the way I played. I did play in a deeper role in midfield, as I was struggling to get up and down the pitch after I got tonsillitis as I couldn't breathe so easily, right up to when I joined Wolves, when I went into a more forward position.

Ernie's third and final Under-23 appearance was on 20 April 1966 in a 2-0 victory against Turkey at Blackburn. After seven minutes a clearance struck George Armstrong and rebounded into the back of the net for a fortuitous opening goal. England should have gone further ahead two minutes after the interval when Ernie put Mick Jones through but, after drawing Artuner, the goalkeeper, he shot wide from six yards. Armstrong's second on the hour was beautifully made and executed, as he sent the ball accelerating past Artuner. Jones and Alan Birchenall, both at Sheffield United at the time, led the line intelligently, but their finishing lacked accuracy. Ernie was described as an 'astute provider' alongside Martin Peters, who in just three months time would grace Wembley in the World Cup final.

Stepney; Badger, Thomson; O'Neil, Cross, Peters; Summerbee, Hunt, Jones, Birchenall, Armstrong.

The game I remember most was against Yugoslavia, which I felt was probably my best match. I tried to give Donald (Rogers) the ball all the time, as I knew what he could do with it. I knew he had great potential and I was trying to help him – that's how I was. I don't remember a lot of the Turkey game, as it

ENGLISH FOOTBALL ASSOCIATION

INTERNATIONAL
UNDER 23

ENGLAND

versus

YUGOSLAVIA

THE DELL

SOUTHAMPTON

kick off 7.30 p.m.

WEDNESDAY

24th NOVEMBER 1965

PROGRAMME PRICE SIXPENCE

Front cover of the programme for England Under-23s *v.* Yugoslavia Under-23s.

was such a big occasion for me and perhaps it went over my head. I was also reserve three times. Alf Ramsey came to see me play when I was at Wolves and I thought I was in with a chance of getting into the full squad. But I did some stupid things in those days and used to play when I wasn't right.

The following season (1966/67) got off to a flying start for Ernie when he scored a brace at Carlisle in September. A free-kick by Mike Bailey in the twenty-third minute evaded the defence to pick out Hugh McIlmoyle. Ernie moved intelligently into position as 'Mack the Knife' edged one of his trademark pin-point headers towards him. Exhibiting fine control, Ernie picked his spot with a meaty low drive past Joe Dean. John Holsgrove ran the ball into the net for Wolves' second six minutes from the interval when Dean failed to reach a threatening cross from Terry Wharton. With forty-nine minutes on the clock Ernie put McIlmoyle away on the right and from the return pass timed his run perfectly to shoot past Dean. Dave Wilson headed a consolation goal for the home side shortly after.

The Blackburn fixture at Molineux the following week rapidly became a contest between steam and electricity, with Ernie's prompting and lightning strikes to the fore as he repeated his two-goal feat. Inside forty-five seconds Ken Knighton won a loose ball in midfield and released Dave Wagstaffe, who beat Billy Wilson and delivered an inch-perfect cross. Ernie, unmarked on the far post, accepted the gift and headed past John Barton. He scored the second in the twenty-fourth minute when a centre from the speedy Terry Wharton flashed across the goalmouth. Wagstaffe, running in from the opposite flank, cracked in a return shot which Barton could only parry and Ernie followed up with a well-placed low hard shot. New signing Dave Burnside ran in to meet an accurate cross from Wharton with a first-time perfect drive in the fiftieth minute for the third, following a timely interception by Joe Wilson. Blackburn imploded with five minutes remaining when Ernie was pulled down by Barton as he surged past David Holt following another McIlmoyle header. Wharton hammered home from the penalty spot. The Wanderers kept the momentum going with a 7-1 victory over Cardiff at Molineux the following week, Terry Wharton scoring a hat-trick and Ernie contributing with a goal and several assists.

On the domestic front Anne watched every game, driving herself to away matches. She was a full-time housewife at their home in Fordhouses, where the Hunts had moved to from Swindon, seemingly spending most of the time cooking for Ernie, who was a steak addict. 'He tucks into steak about four times a week but never eats potatoes,' said Anne at the time, declining to join Ernie in his daily glass of raw egg mixed with sherry. Anne was also learning Spanish in preparation for accompanying Ernie abroad to sell boat trips in Majorca.

Wolverhampton Wanderers 1966/67. From left to right, back row: Farrington, Wagstaffe, Hunt, J. Wilson, Burnside, Wharton, Bailey, L. Wilson. Middle row: Flowers, Dougan, Holsgrove, Parkes, Thomson, Taylor, Davies, Knowles, Woodfield, Buckley. Front row: Dowen (Trainer), Howley (Secretary), Clark (Director), Sproson (Vice-Chairman), Ireland (Chairman), J. Marshall (Director), H. Marshall (Director), Allen (Manager).

Waggy, Bobby Woodruff, Mike Bailey and I all lived on the same estate at Fordhouses. Somebody told me about eating raw eggs and you'll believe anything if you think it's going to make you stronger. I had it for years and still love my steak now. I went on holiday to Majorca for seven or eight years with Anne and the two kids, and we sold boat trips over there one summer. It was set up by a fella I got to know who owned a hotel out there. He got hold of my passport and saw it was Roger Hunt, and of course thought I was Liverpool's Roger Hunt. When we first got there he kept on bringing us bottles of champagne and looking after us as if we were royalty! I couldn't let him go on like that and explained I played football, but wasn't the Roger Hunt he thought I was. He was fine. They had a hotel team that played a couple of games and I remember playing with Keith Morgan once. The hotel owner brought bottles of champagne to the game and all the waiters were pissed and falling all over the place!

In October 1966 Northampton were brushed aside 4-0 at the County Ground. Ernie, switched by Ronnie Allen in a masterstroke from midfield to striker, scored a hat-trick with the ease that suggested Alf Ramsey would not have been wasting his time if he had a look on England's behalf. The previous season Ernie concentrated on scheming behind the attack and he was now acting as a double-striker with Hugh McIlmoyle. Some weeks before the game Allen hung the mantra 'Be Busy' in the dressing room. Ernie took him to heart with three fine opportunist goals, with the fourth a powerful drive by

McIlmoyle, who opened the scoring. Ernie had twin centre halves John Kurila and Don Martin tackling empty air and popped in two goals inside four minutes late in the game. He ghosted into untended pastures for the first as he advanced on Bill Brown after being released by Dave Wagstaffe. Brown attempted a vain sliding tackle outside the penalty area in an effort to stop Ernie as he steered the ball into an empty net. Wolves swarmed all over their opponents and netted the third goal after seventy-eight minutes when Wagstaffe found Terry Wharton on the left. The winger beat Martin and cut inside before passing back to Dave Burnside, who swept the ball into the Cobblers' goalmouth and Ernie arrowed in on goal to score from close range. He completed his hat-trick when Wharton gained possession and fired in a first-time shot which Brown parried brilliantly, but could not hold. Ernie was on hand to whip the ball away from Brown's desperate dive and stab it into the net. Ronnie Allen was delighted: 'This was our best performance of the season. It was the way we played as a team that satisfied me. I thought Hunt looked England class.' The *Daily Express* endorsed Allen's views with the headline, 'Hunt looks right for Ramsey.'

Davies; Wilson, Thomson; Bailey, Woodfield, Flowers; Wharton, Hunt, McIlmoyle, Burnside, Wagstaffe.

Naturals like Ernie strike the ball crisply, instinctively and with unanswerable authority. Nonetheless he worked assiduously on his volleying, was enjoying his football and established a telepathic understanding with Mike Bailey.

In three seasons with Ronnie Allen, the club started the long haul to the top. Ronnie was a lovely man, we used to spend a lot of time after training volleying balls at each other. He obviously had been a very good player and still had a great style to his volleying. Way back at school I used to take all the free-kicks and felt that I could do most things with the ball. Mike Bailey says I was one of the best passers of the ball he had seen and I normally played alongside him in a forward midfield position.

The 1966 players' Christmas party was the perfect stage for Ernie to reveal the extrovert nature of his personality, as reported in the *Birmingham Sports Argus* by an incredulous Ron Flowers. 'The last thing we expected at our Christmas party was a strip show, but that's what we got – and from an unexpected source. There we were enjoying ourselves at the after-dinner dance in which we had invited some friends when these two 'girls' walked in. They did not take much persuading to do their strip act, regardless of the wives and girlfriends who were there. Things went off well, in the literal sense, to reveal our home-made

First step towards a hat-trick for Wolves' inside-forward Ernie Hunt as he sends the ball into the net with Northampton goalkeeper Brown on the ground behind him.

THE WAY TO A HAT-TRICK

Ernie Hunt sits it out, but the ball is safely in the roof of the Northampton goal, from his trusty right foot for the second of his three goals.

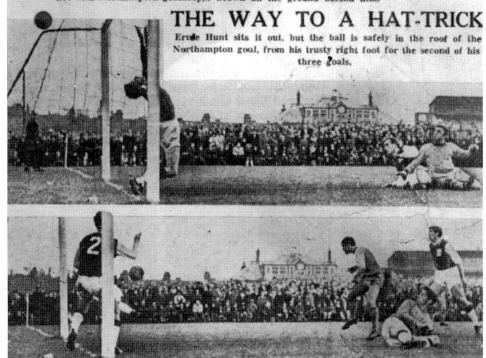

And here's the goal that gave Ernie his first hat-trick for Wolves, the ball beating the two Northampton defenders on the line while goalkeeper Brown can only look around, helpless.

October 1966 – Ernie scores a hat-trick for Wolves against Northampton Town. Top picture: Ernie directs the ball into an empty net with keeper Bill Brown stranded. Middle: Ernie fires in a drive with his right foot from Dave Burnside's cross. Bottom: Ernie poaches the third before Brown can recover.

comedians, Waggy and Ernie. Of the two Dave looked the more realistic as a female impersonator. You could have fooled me when he first walked into the hall, but when Ernie followed I had no doubts!'

We never 'pulled' when Waggy and I dressed up as birds. I was the big bandy one, but nobody tried it on. Ron used to write for the Argus, *as I did. I used to make things up as every Friday the reporter phoned me and asked for a story. I would be trying to get ready for the match the next day and said things like, 'Waggy was locked out of his own house one night so he had to get a ladder, and was going through the bedroom window when the police called round and thought he was burgling the place.' So I had to make sure I told him before the paper came out! I said to him, 'At least you got a mention.'*

Ernie further diversified in 1967 when he took a part-interest with Mike Bailey in 'The Savoury Duck,' a Birmingham city restaurant.

I had the Savoury Duck in Birmingham New Street for a couple of years until I moved to Everton, when I sold out. It was awkward to get there and take an active interest, as we were always playing. I enjoyed it while it lasted and the food they dished up was magnificent.

In February 1967 six players passed fitness tests just before the home game against Bolton. Among them was Ernie who, despite having both thighs heavily strapped, scored twice and made one goal. Wolves suffered an early jolt when Bolton swept into the lead in the first minute, courtesy of Brian Bromley. Following a brilliant run by Terry Wharton soon after, Wolves secured a corner. Wharton's kick was headed goalbound by Dave Woodfield and Ernie, with his back to goal, tamed the ball and, as he fell, turned it wide of Eddie Hopkinson for a deserved equalizer. In the thirtieth minute Wolves went ahead with a superb goal from Bob Hatton, deputizing for the injured Hugh McIlmoyle. The running was made by Peter Knowles and, from Ernie's final pass, Hatton worked his way clear of the defence and beat Hopkinson with a left-foot rocket which hit the net just behind the bar. Wolves increased the lead in the second half when Mike Bailey crossed to Ernie, who almost went on his knees to nod the ball well wide of Hopkinson. Five minutes later Bromley again hauled Bolton back into the game before a second from Hatton and a goal from Dave Wagstaffe saw Wolves home in a thrilling finale. Said a jubilant Ronnie Allen, 'Playing Hunt was a calculated risk but it paid off. He had treatment during the morning but we strapped him up and hoped for the best. I nearly brought him off in the second half, but he stood up to everything so well that I decided to leave him on.'

February 1967 – A classic picture of one of Ernie's great attributes, as he uses his upper-body strength to shield the ball from Everton's John Hurst in the FA Cup fixture.

During the 4-0 win over Hull in March 1967 when Derek Dougan, another shrewd Allen signing, bagged a hat-trick on his home debut, Ernie was forced to leave the field midway through the second half with an injury.

The damage was done at Plymouth the week before. I should have taken a rest, but wanted to play against Hull and did so with the toe strapped up. I was kicked on it in the first five minutes and after that I wasn't much use to the team.

Ronnie Allen said, 'He shouldn't really have played against Hull, but he was so keen we took a chance.' Ernie missed the following three games through injury and marked his return at home to Rotherham in April with a goal in the first minute. Latching on to a suicidal backpass from Chris Rabjohn that never looked like reaching 'keeper Alan Hill, Ernie pounced first and slammed the ball into the net. Wolves experimented with Saturday night soccer and secured

1967 – a portrait of Ernie in Wolves' kit.

the biggest League gate of the day (32,000). They did struggle to negotiate their way through the banks of Rotherham's defensive system, but Derek Dougan wrapped up victory with a superb header from a Dave Wagstaffe cross.

Effervescent Ernie carried his goalscoring form into the following game at Preston. In the second minute Mike Bailey fashioned an incisive pass to Dave Burnside, who clipped a ball skidding through the Preston defence to the receptive feet of Ernie. He outpaced Tony Singleton and Jim McNab before coolly shooting past the advancing Alan Kelly. Four minutes from the interval Wolves deservedly went two ahead from a well-flighted corner on the right by Peter Knowles. Dave Woodfield nodded on and Ernie took Kelly by surprise, whipping the ball into the net with a perfectly executed overhead scissors kick. In the forty-eighth minute Ernie was a mere touch away from a hat-trick. A low Dave Wagstaffe cross into the danger area narrowly eluded him as he crashed into a defender. Ernie Hannigan sparked a revival with a goal after fifty-six minutes but Wolves held on, driven by Mike Bailey's exhorting qualities, as they continued their march towards the First Division.

With one point needed to make absolutely sure of promotion and three games remaining, Wanderers were soon in the ascendancy at Molineux against Bury with an early chance for Derek Dougan, as he rose majestically to head the ball from a corner. With Dougan taking the high ground and the darting Ernie the low ground, the pairing caused chaos in the visiting defence. A quick throw from Phil Parkes to Dave Wagstaffe started the move for the opening goal in the twelfth minute. Dougan released Ernie standing to the left of goal and, as he turned, he was brought down by John Bain in the box. Terry Wharton stepped up to convert with a powerful assured penalty. Six minutes later Dougan made it two when he controlled a probing cross from Wagstaffe, leaving him time to pick his spot with a low drive. It appeared to be another insipid display from the relegation-haunted opposition until they conjured a goal out of the blue from George Jones towards the end of the first half. Indeed Bury looked the livelier side in the early exchanges after the break and a through ball from Bobby Collins found Alex Dawson in the clear. With only Parkes to beat, he miskicked and Bury's chances of salvaging a point evaporated. After fifty-four minutes Ernie headed down to Dave Burnside, who finished with an unstoppable shot. Dougan wrapped up an emphatic victory following another tormenting cross from the left by Wagstaffe. As 'keeper Turner advanced, the 'Doog' unleashed a powerful drive which crashed into the net off the underside of the bar. Promotion was confirmed and, inevitably with an emotional individual like Ernie, tears mixed with cheers as thousands of fans invaded the pitch and stood in the pouring rain to acclaim their team.

Parkes; Taylor, Thomson; Bailey, Hawkins, Holsgrove; Wharton, Hunt, Dougan, Burnside, Wagstaffe. Sub: Knowles.

Norwich were the Wanderers' next victims at Molineux, trounced by the same scoreline with two goals in the opening phase from Derek Dougan, followed by a cross-cum-shot from Terry Wharton that deceived Kevin Keelan in goal. The quality of football was exemplified by the final goal from Ernie in the fifty-sixth minute, which brought the house down. Joe Wilson, in his last appearance for Wolves, overlapped on the right and measured a superb cross into the goalmouth just out of the reach of Keelan. With the Norwich defence split apart, Ernie charged through the middle to head in with a spectacular dive. By the time Tony Woolmer had responded for Norwich towards the end, the game had long ceased to be a contest as the ecstatic crowd celebrated.

At the end of April 1967 Wanderers suffered a setback to clinching the Second Division championship against Coventry City, who had pursued them down the back straight. Itching to reassert their credentials, these two aspiring teams played out an intoxicating drama dubbed the Midlands 'Match of the Century' in front of a record 51,455 Highfield Road crowd. The Wolves fought their hosts for every inch of grass, for every gulp of air during a spiky opening period, but City ultimately ran out 3-1 winners, Peter Knowles scoring the consolation goal. On the final day of the season and requiring just a point to secure the title, Wanderers lost 4-1 at Crystal Palace, letting the honour slip through their fingers because of early defensive mistakes. Palace were two up inside twenty-eight minutes through Danny Light and Bobby Woodruff, returning to haunt his erstwhile employers. Jack Bannister made it three and, while Ernie pulled one back with a brilliant volley, Barry Dyson hammered home Palace's superiority three minutes from time. The defeat allowed fellow contenders Coventry to nudge ahead by a single point.

When I scored that overhead kick at Preston we knew we would go up. After the Bury game when we got back to the dressing room, Mike Bailey and I cried our eyes out, as we realized we had reached our dream of playing in the First Division, and we still had to go back out onto the pitch. Things didn't quite go to plan as we lost at Crystal Palace but, fair play to Coventry, who finished top. They had a good side and their captain George Curtis, who I got to know well later, brought in some bottles of champagne when they beat us at Highfield Road.

While the goalscorers took all the plaudits, Mike Bailey was one of the best wing halves I played with. He was Wolves' Player of the Year that season and Midlands Footballer of the Year, and made the Wolves team that went up tick. Wolves had always been renowned for playing with wide players and we played 4-2-4 with two wingers, Terry Wharton and Dave Wagstaffe, and Peter Knowles up front alongside either Hugh McIlmoyle or the 'Doog'. I sneaked in behind them and scored a few goals. It was quite an adventurous system, but it worked for us as we scored more goals than we conceded.

As if to endorse those comments Ernie enjoyed a superb season, top-scoring with 20 goals in 37 games. During the summer of 1967 Wolves participated in a tournament in the United States, designed to promote professional soccer seriously for the first time in America. Typically the tour was as memorable for Ernie for his off-field activities as the matches he played in:

We arrived at Los Angeles and stayed at the Sheraton West Hotel in Wiltshire Boulevard on Sunset Strip. On our first night Dave Wagstaffe and I wandered out for a drink right in the middle of the city. We couldn't find any pubs and after about half an hour went up the back of a house where we heard some music, as we thought it might be quite promising. We were greeted by a very big coloured man at the top of the stairs, who said to us, 'You paid to come in here? You want some weed? You want a woman?' We didn't realize that we'd got lost and were right in the middle of a black area, the toughest part of LA, a no-go area for whites. We phoned up for a taxi back to our hotel quick!

1967 – Ernie and Wolves skipper Mike Bailey start a school race.

On another night Waggy and I went out, and I pulled this girl. We had already been told if we were in a car not to run into the back of anybody, as it would cost a fortune in insurance because of whiplash. What happens? She drove me back to the hotel and went smack into the back of this car. I was all set to get out of the car and felt a gun, which she was digging into my ribs. She said, 'Don't get out of the car, leave it to me.' The other driver came up to us and said, 'You know what you've done, you've run into the back of my car. You owe me $50.' There was hardly a scratch on the car, but luckily we'd just been paid our expenses for the week. They were in my pocket so, to avoid any hassle or publicity, I thought I'd better pay him quick. It was a bit like a scene out of a movie.

Representing Los Angeles, Wolves played their first match in the Astrodome at Houston against the powerful Bangu of Brazil in front of 35,000 fans. Wanderers should have scored at least five goals, but spurned countless chances and only drew level with a last-minute equalizer from Dave Woodfield. Sports telecaster Chick Hearn, who travelled with the team after the game remarked, 'I've travelled with a lot of pro teams, football, basketball and baseball, but I've never seen or heard anything like this.' He was referring to the sing-song on the bus that started as soon as they left the Astrodome. The ditty about Ernie was a take-off of *The Farmer Takes a Wife* and started, 'Ernie's on the Hunt.' Derek Dougan rendered his edition of *Strangers in the Night* and Ernie was in his element with *I left My Heart in San Francisco*. He was looking forward to playing there, but typically events didn't exactly go to plan.

I got sent off in San Francisco against Ado of Holland in similar circumstances to when I was dismissed for Swindon in Belgium. It was so stupid, one of their blokes was following me all over the pitch kicking lumps out of me and in the end I knocked him out. All the playing staff came on the pitch and when it all blew over, I noticed the bloke I knocked out was lying on the ground and someone had put the trainer's bucket on his head! I was really steaming because he'd been kicking me for nothing, so for the return leg we played our 'keeper Fred Davies at centre forward. I sat on the bench with Tommy Steele, who we had met when seeing him perform Half a Sixpence *with Fred Astaire. Fred went and scored in the game – he was better than me up front – he said I was too small! I could have been a useful centre forward, if we'd found a winger capable of crossing the ball low enough!*

Having won the Western Division League, in the final at the Los Angeles Coliseum in July, Wolves beat Aberdeen 6-5 with 18,000 spectators in attendance. Not many perhaps in a 100,000 stadium, but had the local Dodgers not been playing baseball in front of 50,000 at the same time, they would undoubtedly have enjoyed a bigger gate.

One of the highlights was playing at the fantastic indoor Houston Astrodome on the synthetic grass. We reached the final and played Aberdeen, who were representing Washington D.C. Geraldine Chaplin kicked the match off and an Aberdeen player put through his own goal in the 'sudden death' extra time. They wanted to toss up for the title, but Ronnie Allen insisted that we played on. Davy Burnside scored a hat-trick and, as he ran over to the touchline to celebrate his third goal, he tripped over all the TV cables. He ended up lying on the ground, cables all round him, laughing his head off, it was very funny. Davy had so much skill, you could throw a piece of soap at him in the shower room and he would catch it on his foot, flip it up and balance it on his head. He was a smashing bloke with a dry sense of humour, played wing half in all the games, finished top scorer and was brilliant. Frank Munro also scored a hat-trick for Aberdeen and Wolves signed him soon after.

Dave Wagstaffe ran into an old Mancunian friend of his at Los Angeles, Davy Jones of The Monkees, who were giving a sell-out show at the Hollywood Bowl. Jones gave Waggy a couple of tickets and he took Ernie along. The Monkees

Above: Summer of 1967 – Wolves tour America where the players meet the Monkees. From left to right: Ernie, Terry Wharton, Davy Jones, Dave Wagstaffe, Mike Bailey and Micky Dolenz.

Right: Davy Jones kits out Ernie at Lenny's Boot Parlour in Los Angeles.

Ernie in his new Wolves colours.

invited the whole team to the studios to watch them film their TV series and
Jones also invited Waggy, Ernie and their wives back over for a holiday.

The highlight of our trip socially was when were given three days off and Terry
Wharton, Waggy and I flew to Las Vegas. On the plane we met Clint 'Cheyenne'
Walker, who starred in the classic TV Westerns. He took us to see Ann-Margret's
opening night in cabaret at the Thunderbird. After the show we were invited
to Ann's cocktail party, where we got talking to Trini Lopez, Paul Anka, Andy
Williams, Johnny Carson and Vic Damone, who I gave a couple of tickets for
our final against Aberdeen to. They were all having their photos taken at the
top of the stairs and there was me and Wharty and Waggy. No-one took our
photos! I kissed Ann-Margret – they were all lovely and it was good fun. I
wasn't a gambler, Terry was. I gave him $50 to gamble one night, he came

1967 – Ernie warming up for Wolves.

back with **** all as usual. We sat by the side of the swimming pool the next day. Wharty, who was ginger-haired and fair-skinned, promptly fell asleep. One side of his body was chocolate, the other side white.

I thought football would really take off in America after the tournament as the people were so enthusiastic. In fact when we went to the airport to fly home there were several hundred Yanks there to see us off, and loads of them had tears in their eyes. It was a great tour. For nearly two months seventeen of us had a superb team spirit and comradeship. It had a great influence on the pitch, as we put on some of the best football we'd ever played.

Back home Ernie was involved in an incident that was totally out of character, one he deeply regrets.

My best mate at Swindon was Dave Webb, who lived across the road from me – I used to serve in his dad's pub when I was thirteen. When I was about twenty-two, we went to the Marlborough mop, about twelve miles from Swindon, which was like a big fair. I went with Anne my missus, Dave and another fella. On the way back we stopped at a pub, it was very quiet and was run by an old couple. Just before closing time about eighteen bikers came in. One of them walked up to the bar and shouted, 'Two pints!' He looked at me and said, 'All footballers are poofs.' He was obviously up for a fight and I couldn't be bothered about it but Anne took offence. 'What do you mean?' she said. I said to her, 'Don't say nothing, leave it.' When he was refused a pint and smashed a glass on the table, I thought here we go. They tried to push me out of the pub so that they could have a go at my mate. I managed to wedge my foot in the door, but there was this big gorilla barring the way. I knocked him for six and all hell broke loose. I got kicked to the ground, so my missus phoned the police. I went back into the pub after the bikers had disappeared and Dave had a huge black eye. He was about three years older than me and could normally look after himself, but he'd been beaten up. The one who came to the door did most of the damage and I can still remember this guy's face as if it was yesterday. The copper eventually turned up half an hour later on his own on a bike.

One day when I was playing for Wolves but back in Swindon, a double-decker bus came round the corner. I recognized the twat with the beard, the 'gorilla' was the conductor. I phoned up the bus depot and pretended to be a long-lost relative of his. They told me where he lived, it was in the old town part of Swindon. I went up there in my car and waited until I saw him come out and walk along the road to the pub. I sat outside the pub until he came out, walked up behind him and said, 'I know you, don't I?' He said, 'You what?' Before he could say anything else I battered two bales of shit out of him.

I kept remembering that night when eighteen of them took on my mate in that pub, all on his own. He was the ringleader and a lot bigger than me, but I couldn't stop hitting him. I'd waited a long time for that, about three or four years. He must have wondered what the hell happened, as I was too steamed up to say anything at the time. I feel bad about what I did now, as there was a report in the paper and I think he lost an eye, but at the time I just wanted revenge. It was out of character for me and about the only time in my life I lost my temper.

Seven
Ernie on the Mersey
1967-1968

Ernie scored twice in six League appearances at the start of the 1967/68 season in the First Division before embarking on a new challenge on Merseyside. His last game for Wolves was in a 2-1 away defeat at Tottenham on 6 September 1967, which he marked with a goal. He had an excellent scoring record for a midfielder, finding the net 35 times in 82 outings for the Wanderers. Ernie's goal tally would have been even higher if he had taken penalties for Wolves. However Terry Wharton was the established spot kicker and Ernie was happy to relinquish that duty. It was not even discussed.

Within almost twelve hours of playing against Spurs I travelled to Goodison and signed for Everton on the dotted line. Just five minutes after I left our Fordhouses home to drive up to meet their manager Harry Catterick, a gypsy called at our front door. Anne crossed her palm with five bob and had her fortune told. The gypsy said we would be travelling and that we would be coming into money. And she added that we would be having a new car and three children. She was right on three counts – we travelled, I did get a signing-on fee and I changed my car, but we had just the two children. Anne and I were very happy in the Midlands, but an offer like the one from Everton comes only once in a lifetime, and if I had said 'No' I would probably have regretted it for the rest of my life. I regarded the move as a tremendous challenge and understood I would be playing a striking role.

The notoriously secretive Harry Catterick said of the deal, 'I was practically certain that I had signed Hunt, but I dared not say anything as I knew at least three other clubs fancied him. It isn't often a player of his calibre becomes available. We have had him covered by our scouting system for a long time and, with his ability to play anywhere in the front line, he will be very valuable to us.'

When I went there, Ronnie Allen wanted me to make a few bob out of the move. Everton had offered £80,000, so Wolves had doubled their money in two

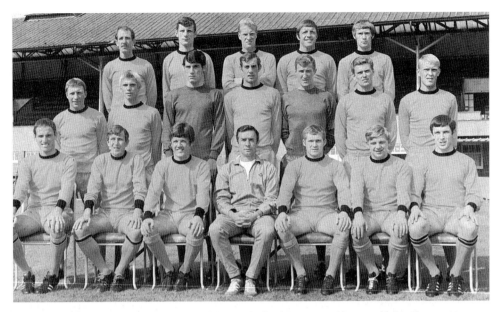

Wolverhampton Wanderers 1967/68. From left to right, back row: Burnside, Woodfield, Flowers, Hunt, Wagstaffe. Middle row: Bailey, Evans, Parkes, Holsgrove, Davies, Thomson, Hawkins. Front row: Dougan, Wilson, Knowles, Allen (Manager), Wharton, Buckley, Taylor.

years. He said he didn't want me to go, but they had young Alun Evans in the reserves coming through popping them in and I thought a move there was my best chance to get an England cap. I talked terms with them, they said they would pay me the tax on the money they spent on me, which was £1,500. They put me in a hotel in Southport when I first got there. It was full of old people, I think they were trying to keep me out of trouble! I sat by the fire on my own when this bloke walked in with a flat hat and an old grey mac up to his neck. He looked around and said, 'Are you Ernie Hunt?' I thought he was play-acting and started to act back. He got out of his pocket a wad of notes, gave them to me and shot out of the room. I never found out who he was or saw him again, it was like something out of a movie.

Twenty-two-year-old Ernie signed for Everton on 8 September 1967 and made his debut in a 2-1 defeat at Fulham the following day, replacing Joe Royle. In November the Hunts moved from their Wolverhampton home to Southport. While it was regarded as a shrewd purchase, it was a mere six-month sojourn for Ernie, who played 14 League games (plus 2 as sub) for the Toffeemen, scoring three times, against Southampton, West Bromwich Albion and Manchester City. He also played in the League Cup home defeat against Sunderland in October 1967. It was always going to be difficult to establish himself in the first team as Ernie was competing for the number eight shirt,

1967/68 – Ernie was only at Everton for six months. These shots are rare ones taken in the colours of the Toffeemen.

which was Alan Ball's, the number four, filled by Howard Kendall and the number nine (Joe Royle) and ten shirts (John Hurst). Harry Catterick did however select him in all these positions. Yet Ernie, dubbed 'Farmer' on Merseyside for his West Country accent, had all the natural ability to become a lasting Everton star. However at Goodison, where perhaps he did not revel in the manager's strongly disciplined methods, he did not settle before being sold at a £10,000 loss. His final appearance was in the FA Cup fifth round 2-0 victory over Tranmere Rovers on 9 March 1968.

I think that Everton had tracked me ever since they beat Swindon in the FA Cup in 1963. They recognized I could score goals and my third game for Everton was in the derby at Anfield. It was a fantastic experience and I never met anything so fanatical in my whole career. It was also the first derby match for Howard Kendall and Emlyn Hughes and, although we lost 1-0, I still enjoyed it.

I felt that by signing for Everton at the time, I might have a shout of getting into the England squad for Mexico 1970, but I never thought I had the opportunity to prove what I was capable of. It was strange, Everton spent all that money on me and didn't seem to know where to play me. Perhaps Catterick never wanted me in the first place, so he put me on the wing. I didn't have much to do with him, but the way he played me out wide didn't seem right. I was never the quickest of players, although I was sharp over ten yards and I could cross a ball. Neither was I very good at dribbling or ever a long runner, I used to play with my head. I could hold people off, but that wasn't what was needed playing out wide. I used to come in and say to Harry, 'This is no good to me, boss.' He would reply, 'Yes, you're right Ernie,' but the next game he would play me in the same position. I needed to be in the thick of things, but I didn't get a chance and in the end I wasn't even getting first-team football. Joe Royle had just come into the side and could knock them down, which would have been ideal for me and was how it worked with Hugh McIlmoyle and the 'Doog' at Wolves, and Jack Smith at Swindon.

I always enjoyed training and loved sessions on the beach at Formby, but Catterick was a strict disciplinarian. We actually had to sign in when we arrived for training – it didn't worry me as I was always there on time, but I never experienced having to 'clock in' at any other club. It was the hardest training I'd ever experienced, more running than any of my other clubs. I think I was actually overtrained with all the running. It didn't make me play or feel better, as my game was all based on the short, sharp movement.

I used to have a few drinks in the social club at Formby. In fact I played for the pub team once and when Catterick found out, he went berserk! I had some fun up there with characters like 'Bally' and Howard Kendall. Alan and I had been having a couple of drinks at a hotel in Southport one evening, when a few rugby players turned up and started taking the piss. Bally challenged one of them to run along the seafront at Southport and back for a fiver. Bally came jogging in with the rugby player nowhere in sight. He was so fit he could run all day and made sure he won, as there was a bit of pride at stake.

Anne and I went on holiday to Majorca with Alan and Lesley Ball one summer in the late sixties. Bally and I went out one night on our own for a few drinks to a bar, it was about four miles from our hotel. We got talking to a couple of Everton fans, who took us to a club. There was a bit of a fracas there, as some people recognized Bally and this bloke had a go at him. I weighed in and smacked him in the face, he went down and all hell let loose. Someone had a go at me and broke my nose. I didn't know where Bally was, but I managed to get away and caught a taxi back to the hotel. I went down to his room and he was there. He'd run all the way back to the hotel and beaten me in my taxi! The next day my face was a mess, but it wasn't the first time my nose had been broken. At the last count I've broken it four times on the pitch and three times off, hence the Jack Bodell profile!

The Everton supporters were good to me – their humour is unbelievable. During one game someone threw me a banana as I had bandy legs and always had a good tan on me. So I peeled it, ate half of it and threw the other half back into the crowd and they applauded.

Not content with starring in one BBC film when at Swindon, Ernie also appeared in another production, this time directed by Ken Loach called *The Golden Vision*. It was a drama-documentary based on the rivalry between the two sets of supporters in Liverpool. There are some marvellous scenes in the film, including a group of working-class Evertonians going down to London for a match at Arsenal in the back of a furniture van. It also features two ladies chatting on their doorsteps, agreeing that there are 'only two teams in Liverpool, Everton and Everton reserves!'

The title came from Alex Young's nickname. Ken Jones, the actor who played Alex, was supposed to jump up and head the ball into the goal. We went for ages while he tried to head it into the net and when he eventually did they'd run out of film and we had to do it again!

Everton was the one club Ernie played for during his prime and did not succeed – a case, perhaps of making the right move at the wrong time. Having arguably made a greater impact as a dressing-room raconteur, it was clear that opportunity on the pitch was restricted on Merseyside and Ernie was soon looking for a further move.

I obviously wasn't happy being a fringe first-team player and had a chat about it after the Tranmere cup game with Maurice Setters, who was at Coventry. I decided to phone Coventry up and actually spoke to the manager Noel Cantwell. He seemed interested in me, but Everton wanted £90,000 at the start. They reduced their fee to £70,000, which was acceptable to Coventry, so I got myself a move there. It gave me the opportunity of staying in the First Division and playing regular first-team football.

Eight

A New Challenge with the Sky Blues: 1968-1970

The transfer of Ernie and Chris Cattlin from Huddersfield Town in March 1968 injected much needed blood into Coventry City's fight against relegation. They both signed on transfer deadline day at a combined cost of £140,000. It was felt by some that Ernie had yet to entirely fulfil the promise he'd shown when he first made the grade with Swindon. A lot of people were ready to write him off after his failure at Goodison and, on the face of it, moving to a new club who were struggling at the time like City didn't help.

They were a great bunch of lads at Highfield Road. Directly I met them I was taken with the friendly, happy attitude. You could sense that they really wanted to go places.

City had struggled to find their feet – with just three League wins by the turn of the year, they lay twentieth, one place above the trapdoor and relegation stared the Sky Blues in the face. When Ernie made his debut with Chris Cattlin on 16 March 1968 against Manchester United, he also set a unique record of playing for three First Division clubs in one season.

City had other problems to contend with. Ten days before the game, fire gutted the central section of Highfield Road's main stand. A rickety temporary stand enabled all the season ticket holders to be accommodated. By kick-off 47,111 bodies had crammed into the stadium – the second highest gate of all time at Highfield Road. The atmosphere was electric and against all the odds City rose above themselves like a phoenix from the ashes of the burnt-out stand. Ten minutes from the interval Willie Carr found Ernie Machin, who rocketed a thirty-yard first-time half-volley past Alex Stepney to open the scoring. Then eight minutes after half-time, Maurice Setters headed in Ernie Hannigan's inswinging corner from close range. United roused themselves, driven on by John Fitzpatrick, who tested Bill Glazier, and Bobby Charlton was denied what looked like a blatant penalty when Ernie clumsily brought him down from behind. City's defence held out to earn a merited victory and a vital

1968 – Ernie relaxing at home in musical mood.

boost for morale. The tall, polished Cattlin shackled George Best, who rarely escaped his attentions. The 'bustling' Ernie slotted in well alongside Machin, supporting the dangerous Neil Martin, while Willie Carr buzzed in his usual manner. Notwithstanding United had endured a 4,000-mile European trip to Poland in midweek, City were finally competing with the best club football had to offer in England and the win was felt by many to mark a watershed in the progress of the club.

Glazier; Bruck, Cattlin; Machin, Setters, Clements; Hannigan, Hunt, Martin, Tudor, Carr.

Ernie's first City goal was in the next game at Roker Park against Sunderland. After Malcolm Moore had given Sunderland the lead, City emerged from a keenly contested duel with honours even when Ernie ghosted on to a John Tudor flick from Dave Clements' free-kick thirteen minutes from time. As he curved it with the outside of his boot, Jim Montgomery was deceived by the swerve of the ball and belatedly dived as it slid inside the right-hand post. Working hard to regain match fitness, Ernie was described in one national newspaper as 'The Mighty General.'

The final game of the season in May 1968 was at Southampton, with City clinging to the First Division by their fingertips and needing at least a point to survive. Seven thousand City fans roared their team on to another backs-to-the-wall display. A muddy surface made football difficult, but City chased, worked and harassed. In a nail-biting final twenty minutes they slowed it down as the players heard that Chelsea were winning at Sheffield United to send them down to the Second Division. Substitute Ernie took the ball on more than one occasion into the opposing corner and held it while precious seconds ticked away. The Sky Blues were indebted to Maurice Setters, nursing four stitches in a cut left eyebrow, with a heroic assured contribution, full of timing and good positioning. He marked Ron Davies out of the game as City fought for their lives to achieve a goalless draw and avoid relegation by a point. Relieved supporters invaded the pitch when the final whistle blew, but Ernie alleges the match result was never in doubt:

A local millionaire businessman got me to bribe four of the Southampton players a 'grand' each if they lost. The phone went and I thought it was a wind-up to start with, but this guy came over as if he knew what was going on and had a good knowledge of the game. I spoke to Anne about it, but not to any Coventry players, I took it on myself without telling anyone else. I didn't even ask him what there was in it for me, as I already had a clause in my contract when I signed for Coventry that I would be paid £2,000 if we stayed

March 1968 – Ernie's first goal for Coventry at Sunderland, as he shrugs off the challenge of Calvin Palmer to fire home.

up anyway. The players I approached all agreed straightaway: four of them, for £1,000 each.

It was a 0-0 draw, we just stayed up and the businessman didn't have to pay anyone. However he also got me to ring one of the Chelsea lads I knew and offer their players £50 each to beat Sheffield United – in those days a win bonus was only worth about £4. Whether the player did in fact make the offer and if so whether it was acted upon by any of the others I shall never know. It was their last game of the season and they had nothing to play for, but they beat them and United were relegated. I wasn't sure what business the millionaire had, but he said it would have lowered his profile if Coventry had got relegated.

Ernie had graduated from the school of hard knocks, learning at an early stage to work hard and play hard. With his outgoing personality, he revelled in his role as cheerleader on trips abroad, although after one particularly gruelling night's journey into day there were some anxious moments:

In 1968 we went on a pre-season tour to Holland, which Noel had to interrupt as he returned home to sign Eric McManus, so Jimmy Andrews the coach, took over. One night Maurice Setters, Ian Gibson and myself went down to this club

Ernie in Coventry City colours.

Coventry City 1968/69. From left to right, back row: Clements, Martin, Bruck, Setters, Tudor, Coop. Middle row: Shepherd, Hill, Curtis, Glazier, Cattlin, Blockley, Kearns. Front row: Hannigan, Gibson, Carr, Cantwell (Manager), Baker, Hunt, Machin.

for a few drinks, not too much as we were playing the next day. This bloke got talking to us and bought us some drinks. On the way back to our hotel he crashed his car, so we had to find our own way back. The next evening after the match we got arrested, as he said we had driven his car. We were taken to the police station and interrogated under spotlights, it looked really serious as they took our passports off us. I have no idea why he claimed that, but halfway through the night we were released without explanation. Apparently when Noel returned he said to Jimmy, 'I've signed Eric.' Jimmy replied, 'I've got a bit of bad news for you.' Noel couldn't believe it, but was all right when we explained what had happened.

City were desperate to avoid the feel of relegation lapping at their ankles again the following season (1968/69), but the omens didn't look good when Neil Martin was ruled out with injury until November. In an attempt to beef up the attack, Noel Cantwell bought Tony Hateley from Liverpool for £80,000. Unfortunately his time at Highfield Road was not fruitful and Hateley was consigned to the reserves when Martin returned. The foil for the strikers was again the impish Ernie, whose alchemist's touch had returned. City gained their first points of the season at the expense of FA Cup holders West Brom in a decisive 4-2 victory. Noel Cantwell raved afterwards about the display of Ian Gibson, the fans' hero, who had been omitted from the first two games of the season. Although Gibson was the architect of the win, the match was also a personal triumph for Ernie with a hat-trick. The die was cast as early as the second minute, when Gerry Baker was adjudged to have been fouled by Doug Fraser and John Kaye simultaneously inside the Albion penalty area. Up stepped Ernie calmly to put City ahead. Shortly after Gibson caught the Albion defence out of position with a thirty-five-yard ball from wide on the left to allow Ernie to head home for the second as 'keeper Rick Sheppard groped the air. Ernie completed his hat-trick in the twenty-fifth minute with a jinking run after Gibson again opened up the defence. After sixty-four minutes Ernie Machin anticipated a move on the right initiated by John Tudor and scored with a powerful shot that Sheppard was unable to hold. Albion replied through former City favourite Ronnie Rees and Tony Brown. It was to be one of the few occasions that season City fans were able to sit back, relax and enjoy the spectacle.

Glazier; Bruck, Cattlin; Machin, Setters, Hill; Hunt, Gibson, Baker, Tudor, Clements.

I loved it at Coventry but I was dropping deeper into midfield and also playing wider, which meant I was not getting enough of the ball. Before the team meeting at the hotel I asked Noel to give me a free role in the West Brom match just behind Neil Martin. I had to get weighed on the morning of the match and as usual I was nearly 13 stone, but as I pushed the weights down, it registered 12 stone 3 pounds. Within twenty-five minutes I had scored a hat-trick and also hit the crossbar. After the game Noel said, 'I told you that was your best weight!' I heard that a Crystal Palace scout was watching me in that game. Bert Head was managing Palace by then and wanted to arrange a swap with Steve Kember. I was doing okay at Coventry up to then but of course, after the West Brom game, it all took off and City didn't want to sell me.

I wanted to play inside behind the front man, like Paul Scholes, where I had already played at Swindon. That convinced them to let me play in that sort of free role, where I could find space by drifting out wide as well as in the middle before the days of overlapping full-backs. I played in that role for four out of six seasons and used to get about fourteen or fifteen goals a season, which wasn't too bad. I don't like to blow my own trumpet, but I knew what I was doing on the pitch and seemed to do it instinctively. People said I had an old head on young shoulders, then as I got older I played even more with my head. I was never a long-distance runner, but I was quick off

August 1968 – Ernie scores the first goal of a hat-trick against West Bromwich Albion with a penalty after just two minutes of the game. Rick Sheppard is the beaten Baggies 'keeper.

the mark and able to see a situation as it developed. I was a thoughtful player, always running between two players when tracking back to prevent them passing, and used my head. I scored in every side I played in, except Everton, not as an out-and-out striker, but coming through from midfield. Playing from midfield I used to be up and down all the game and at Coventry had a telepathy with two Scots in particular, Ian Gibson and Willie Carr. They seemed to be able to read my mind and knew when I needed the ball.

In September 1968 Ernie and Anne completed their second house move in less than twelve months. They moved from Formby to the Finham district of Coventry. At the end of the month Anne opened a new boutique in Swindon with Jean Williams, the wife of Ernie's friend Gerry, called The Clothes Peg. Ernie went to a club in Bristol on one occasion with Gerry and some friends, and was asked to go on stage with Roy Castle. Never one to hold back, Ernie walked on stage, sat on his lap, started an impromptu ventriloquist act and stole the show.

A miserable first half to the season meant an upward battle in the New Year. To their credit, City scraped five draws and in the last eleven games secured

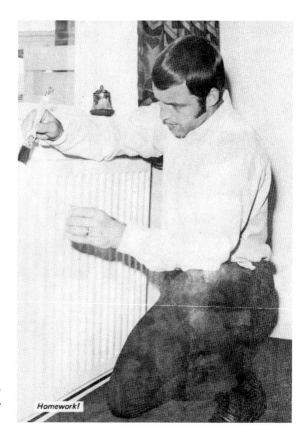

Homework!

1968 – a domesticated Ernie brushing up on his painting skills (*left*) and cutting the grass (*below left*).

September 1968 – Ernie manages a trademark volley in the League Cup victory over Portsmouth, despite the close attention of Tommy Youlden.

overdue victories against Burnley, Leicester and Manchester United to survive, again finishing just one point above relegated Leicester City. Ernie was virtually an ever-present, but jeopardized his record in March 1969 when determined to watch the team he supported as a boy in the League Cup final.

Ernie invited Gerry Williams and two other mates to watch City play West Ham in a Friday night game at Upton Park. Coventry were defeated 5-2 and after scoring one of the goals with a volley, Ernie was taken off injured. Skipper George Curtis told Ernie he was to go back on the team bus for treatment, but he would have none of it. He jumped off the coach, unwrapped the bandages on his leg and said to Gerry, 'I'm coming with you lads to watch Swindon at Wembley.' They stayed in London overnight and the next day drove down Wembley Way in a taxi with Ernie waving to the crowd! His day was complete when Swindon defeated hot favourites Arsenal.

I was injured during the West Ham game and should have gone in for treatment on the Saturday. However I wanted to watch Swindon at Wembley with my mates. We played out a draw against Stoke a couple of days later,

A smiling Ernie poses for the camera.

which I just about managed to get through. I was substituted in the next game against Burnley and made out I was injured in the Stoke game, but really I never recovered from the West Ham match.

Ernie finished top scorer in his first full season for the Sky Blues with 13 goals, missing just three games. Derrick Robins, the City chairman, rewarded his team with a trip to Barbados for their efforts in escaping relegation. Ernie was always going to make the most of his first holiday in the Caribbean:

We went to Bermuda and Barbados, where George Curtis was in charge of the beer – he used to think he was the landlord of the pub. One night we went down to a bar in town where we sat down in a circle and these naked women *came out and sat on our laps. When two birds came out dancing, Maurice Setters and I got up to dance with them. I'd had a few drinks as usual and said to one of them, 'I'll see you afterwards, you come back to our hotel?' All the lads were chanting 'Ernie' and the bird took off her bikini bottom to reveal this black d**k hanging down! We'd been stitched up rotten!*

One day we kept George talking outside the front of the room where we kept the beers so I could sneak in the back. I had locked the back door and put the key outside, so I knew we could get back in and have a few more beers later. When we got back we had a bottle-walking competition, stretching out with your arms to see how far you could put forward a bottle, then come back. When it was my turn I slipped and the bottle broke and cut my nose. I made my way to my beach chalet and just got in when George turned up. 'I knew it was you,' he said. He'd followed the spots of blood right from the room, round the swimming pool to our chalet. I was drinking with Brian Hill and Bill Glazier, who could drink a pint quicker than I could drink a large vodka. He had hollow legs, mind you he was a brilliant goalkeeper who was so unlucky not to play for England, but he could definitely drink for England!

The day before we played a Barbadian team, about half a dozen of us went out to one of the beautiful beaches. We took seven bottles of Mateus Rose with us. Willie Carr and myself drew the short straws to go to the local supermarket to buy another twenty-one bottles. The sun was shining and we weren't worried about going to training that day, so we decided on a little game. You had to drink one bottle straight down and make a little speech. Everyone managed the first and by the time we'd finished, all the bottles had been drunk. Everyone was slagging off the manager, but 'deadpan' Brian Hill said, 'I hope we have a safe journey home.' Young Trevor Shepherd disappeared and we eventually found him curled up in the toilet of the beach bar fast asleep! Then in the distance we saw a canoe paddling towards us – it was George Curtis, who had been out looking for us. He drew up on the beach and said, 'You're back in ****ing training in two hours time!' You didn't argue with 'Iron Man' George, talk about 'Sanders of the River,' that was George. He used to give me a love bite when we played away. Anne would say, 'Don't give me that!' Of course George would deny it when he saw her.

Maurice Setters and I signed for all the bottles of drink and champagne in Dave Clements' name, as he had a bit of a reputation for being tight-fisted. But at the end of the trip Noel, who knew Maurice well, having played with him at Manchester United, said, 'I recognize your handwriting.' So instead of a fine we had to pay the money back – it was about £250.

In 1969/70 Noel Cantwell consciously played a more defensive system in an effort to avoid a relegation battle for a third consecutive year. The traditional air

Coventry City 1969/70. From left to right, back row: Martin, Cattlin, Hateley, Glazier, Curtis, McManus, Blockley, Hill, Coop. Middle row: Setters, Hannigan, Bruck, Gibson, Cantwell (Manager), Machin, Clements, Hunt. Front row: Paddon, Carr, Baker.

of optimism accompanying a new season was matched by the hope that Cantwell had fashioned a side more difficult to beat, with the backbone of Glazier, Setters or Curtis and Ernie and Neil Martin up front. Youngsters from the youth team were starting to blossom, notably Dennis Mortimer and Jeff Blockley. After missing the start of the season Ernie entered the fray at the end of August 1969 for the Highfield Road fixture against Wolves. This was Ernie country, relishing the opportunity to put one over his old teammates and his strike after fifty-four minutes was the defining moment of the match. There seemed little danger when Jeff Blockley hit a long ball from the halfway line to the edge of the penalty area. Ernie challenged for the ball in the air and, as the ball dropped, he swivelled and struck a sumptuous volley with his right foot inside the far post past the despairing dive of Phil Parkes. In a hard, physical battle City held firm, kept their shape and discipline, and were worthy recipients of a sustained standing ovation at the final whistle.

In October 1969 the cheek of City's showman decided the away game at Arsenal. In the thirty-first minute Dave Clements clipped the ball back from the goal line to the receptive Ernie, who dummied Jon Sammels perfectly and crashed home a low drive past debutant 'keeper Geoff Barnett from the edge of the box. It was a historic first victory over Arsenal as Ernie continually danced around the Gunners' defence. Four days later Noel Cantwell took his team to

Right: September 1969 – Ernie salutes his goal against Leeds. He is embraced by Neil Martin.

Below: October 1969 – Ernie is foiled by Geoff Barnett this time, but had the last laugh as he scored the only goal of a historic first victory against Arsenal at Highbury. Sandwiched in between are Peter Simpson and Peter Storey.

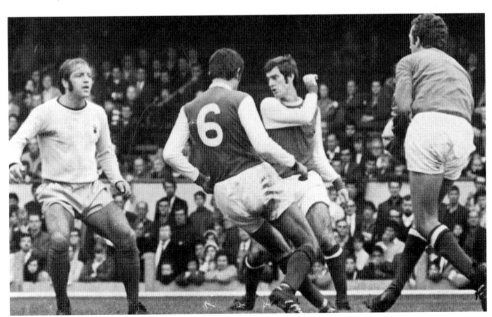

the Baseball Ground, where the Sky Blues secured an extraordinary 3-1 victory, defeating a Derby side unbeaten in twenty-five home games. Even County manager Brian Clough acknowledged the performance as brilliant.

Noel Cantwell strengthened the side further with the signings of striker John O'Rourke and defender Roy Barry, marking the start of a run of eight wins and a draw in ten matches, which took City to the previously uncharted heights of fourth place. The change of tactics was so successful that City took the Division by storm to finish in sixth place, gaining entry into the Fairs Cup for the first time in their history. Ernie took enormous satisfaction in seeing City achieve their European dream with a 0-0 draw at Wolves in April 1970 and his personal contribution was 9 goals from 34 appearances.

That season we had the benefit of a good start and found our confidence again, and results started to go our way. The previous season when we nearly got relegated, we played some good stuff, but every game was like a cup final. We were too anxious, there were too many defeats by the odd goal and our confidence slumped. We became a much more fluid team and if we had been a bit tougher, like Leeds, we could have been even more successful. Roy Barry made a tremendous difference to our defence until he broke his leg. We stopped giving away silly goals and were sharper up front. We were knocked out of both cup competitions early and that gave us the chance to concentrate on strengthening our League position.

In May 1970 City went on a summer tour to USA. The trip started in St Louis, where City lost 2-1 to a goal in the last minute. Neil Martin was the Coventry scorer and Ernie came on as substitute for Billy Rafferty after sixty-five minutes. City moved on to play Kansas City Spurs, where they secured a 3-1 win, Ernie scoring the opening goal for City with a fierce shot from twenty-five yards. Ernie played in the next five matches, four of which City won, before being dropped for the last match of the tour against Rochester Lancers, which the Sky Blues won 2-1. Neil Martin and Dietmar Bruck were other notable absentees:

We went to America as a reward for getting Coventry into Europe for the first time. All the lads had a few drinks on the plane, although we were playing at St Louis the next day. We got there at about eight and were invited to a cocktail reception. I was rooming with Bobby Gould's brother Trevor, and Ernie Machin was rooming with Mick Coop. Ernie and Mick came into our room on the twelfth floor, as they were dying for something to eat. Ernie rang down to room service for some food to be brought up to us. We waited over an hour, but they were so knackered they gave up and went to their room on

December 1969
– Ernie fires
home the first
goal of a 3-0
victory at Crystal
Palace.

*about the eighteenth floor. It was about 4 a.m. and we were just nodding off when there was a knock on our door and a huge coloured gentleman arrived with a massive trolley of food. He wheeled it in and I phoned through to Ernie and Mick, but there was no reply. I went into the corridor to wheel the trolley to the lift, without any clothes on, but I must have hit the wall, as the food went all over the floor. I started to pick it up and put it back on the trolley, when the lift opened and Noel Cantwell came out! He looked at me and said, 'Ernie, what the ****ing hell are you doing?' I replied, 'Room service boss!' I can see his face now as he tried to control himself. He told me later he didn't know how he could contain himself at the time.*

Willie Carr and I went out drinking one evening and Willie phoned his wife Tess when he got back to the hotel. He laid on his bed and cut short the call as he had to go to the bathroom as he wasn't feeling too bright, so he put the phone down. When he got back to the bedroom he crashed out on the bed and fell asleep. He went down the next day to reception and found out he'd been charged about $90 for the call, as the phone was still off the hook.

At the end of the tour we stayed in Rochester, New York. The night before we were due to play against a college team, Neil Martin and I went out for a few drinks. It was quite late, but when we got back we went to his room for a drink. Neil was rooming with Dietmar Bruck, who told us he was going over to visit some relatives of his. Dietmar put all the pillows under his blanket to make it look like he was in bed in case Norman Pilgrim, the physio, checked up on us. We'd got hold of a load of swords, like you put in cocktails, and stuck them all into Dietmar's pillows to make it look like he'd been stabbed. Soon after I went back to my room and just missed Noel, who went round to Neil's room and said, "Where have you been?" 'I've just been out for a few drinks, boss,' said Neil. 'And where's Dietmar?' 'He's been stabbed, boss!' The next morning Noel said to Neil and I, 'You're not going to the do tonight, you're not playing and furthermore you're getting a $50 fine.' About two hours later Norman brought my jersey round, did the same for Neil, then an hour later he rushed back and took our jerseys off us. So they went off to play while Neil and I went swimming in the pool!

We used to call Norman Pilgrim 'Djalmar Santos' after the great Brazilian footballer – he loved that, as he thought he could play a bit. When we got to the airport on our way back to England, we put out a call for 'Mr Djalmar Santos from Coventry City' – you should have seen his face.

Nine

Goal of the Season
1970-1971

Of all the images imprinted on the mind from the 1970s, one of the most enduring occurred when Ernie gained lasting fame for the enterprising two-footed 'donkey flick' free-kick he perfected with Willie Carr in October 1970 at Highfield Road against Everton. With ten minutes remaining the Sky Blues were leading the League Champions 2-1, when a free-kick was awarded in a central position on the edge of the penalty area. Carr stood over the ball, trapped it between his heels and flicked it up vertically. As it fell, Ernie hammered a perfect right-foot dipping volley over the wall and into the top corner of Andy Rankin's goal. The crowd went wild. The *Match of the Day* cameras captured it all and ensured its place in folklore, and it was voted Goal of the Month and Goal of the Season. Eleven million television viewers saw the free-kick, which remains one of the most remarkable goals ever seen at Highfield Road.

Glazier; Coop, Bruck; Clements, Blockley, Strong; Hunt, Carr, Martin, O'Rourke, Alderson.

The *Sunday Telegraph* described it as one of the highlights of the weekend's TV viewing. Harry Catterick was less generous – 'Like something out of a circus,' he grumbled. Any résumé of football in the seventies has to include a re-run of the classic moment conjured up by the City pair. Ernie's memory of the goal that guaranteed him recognition to a whole generation of fans is vivid.

I was in charge of the free-kicks at Coventry and we were told about the 'donkey' kick by coach Bill Asprey, who had seen something similar at Lilleshall. Willie and I had practised it in training and at half-time Noel Cantwell wanted to know why we hadn't attempted it in the first half when we got a free-kick in a good position. I told him I wanted to wait until the kick was in the dead centre.

We were awarded a free-kick just outside the penalty area in the second half and I waited patiently for Everton to build their defensive wall. I thought

Coventry City 1970/71. From left to right, back row: O'Rourke, Parker, Coop, Gould, Hunt, Bruck. Middle row: Mortimer, Hill, Glazier, Joicey, McManus, Rafferty, Blockley. Front row: Machin, Cattlin, Barry, Cantwell (Manager), Martin, Clements, Carr.

about slipping it through Willie's legs for Dave Clements to blast it, but decided to give the donkey kick a crack. Willie stood over the ball with it wedged between his ankles. He flicked it up with a backward donkey-style flip of both feet. As the ball came down I smacked it on the volley with my right foot, and the ball flashed high into the Everton net with Andy Rankin stranded the wrong side of his line.

When it went in, I felt a mixture of emotions, surprise and fear, after I realized what I had done. Willie was so excited, but I was trying to keep my hair in decent shape, as everyone was hugging and kissing me in front of the cameras! The crowd went quiet before erupting, then I was aware of a buzz going round the ground of people talking about the goal. People tend to forget I scored another goal earlier in the game. Brian Alderson, wide on the left wing, cut inside and hit it just outside the area. It smacked the post and spun out, and I managed to keep it down and score.

If I'd had royalties for every time the goal has been shown on the television since then, I'd be a millionaire by now, but that sort of thing has never bothered me. I honestly couldn't believe the impact it would have.

Andy Rankin recalls the goal: 'I remember bobbing up and down to try and get a clear view of the free-kick, as we had four men in the wall. I saw Willie Carr flick the ball up and then caught Ernie volley it. As it came towards me, I thought that's going in and realized there was nothing I could do about it. It was a quality strike and a great goal. Of course if I'd have saved it, it might not have even been shown on *Match of the Day* and achieved fame and notoriety in the way it did, so perhaps Ernie has a lot to thank me for!'

The Everton match was not the first or last time the manoeuvre was attempted. Ernie's mistimed effort in a friendly away to Blackpool almost hit the corner flag, but soon after the youth team emulated their effort.

We tried it during pre-season at Blackpool, but it nearly hit the hands of the clock on the tower! We also tried it against Tottenham later in the season (April 1971) when Pat Jennings was in goal. It hit the crossbar and was the last time we did it. We were obviously delighted with it, but there was a protest from Scottish referees who watched it on the television. They said it was illegal as the ball couldn't be played with both feet at once from a free-kick. A complaint went to FIFA and they banned it. It seemed ridiculous to outlaw something so inventive.

October 1970 – Ernie shapes up to volley home the famous 'donkey' free-kick against Everton at Highfield Road.

Life did not get much better for Coventry fans than in that first weekend in October. The victory over Everton, who had won their previous six games, came the day after City had been drawn against Bayern Munich in the Fairs Cup. The city was buzzing with the expectation of witnessing a team that boasted a formidable backbone of Franz Beckenbauer, Gerd Müller and Sepp Maier. The Sky Blues embarked on their maiden cruise to Europe with a comfortable win over Bulgarian side Trakia Plovdiv in the first round. For the first leg in Munich, City were weakened by the absence of Bill Glazier, who was replaced by tyro 'keeper Eric McManus. In a dispiriting ninety minutes Munich were in no mood for mercy and were four goals to the good after twenty minutes. At one moment City did seem to have a chance when Ernie's flying header from a cross made it 1-1. However two goals from Schneider and one each from Schwarzenbach and Muller ended the argument. In the second half Roth and Muller made it half a dozen and, whilst City fought bravely to the end, there was no relief for them. The waterlogged pitch certainly made life difficult for goalkeepers, as the third and fifth goals dipped under McManus, who dived fractionally too late. City were well beaten in midfield and the German side were in a different class, Beckenbauer strolling through the game.

Beckenbauer was marking me, but I managed to score after ten minutes, then I hit the crossbar and the post. In the second half it started raining and Schneider was firing them from about thirty yards out. They were hitting the floor and bouncing over Eric's dive. How can you knock such an inexperienced 'keeper, who went on to have a decent career with Stoke? On the plane back Ernie Machin said in a deadpan voice, 'Well, if you were flying this plane Eric, you'd drop the controls and we'd all be dead!' We were just trying to make a joke of it and Eric did have a sense of humour. He was a lovely lad and I really felt for him.

The home leg, originally earmarked as a potential 50,000 all-ticket extravaganza, was watched by barely half that number. City did regain some respectability as Neil Martin and John O'Rourke scored in a 2-1 success. After the euphoria of the previous season, Noel Cantwell again had problems in identifying the right blend to lead City's attack throughout the campaign. The Martin-O'Rourke combination failed to live up to expectations and goals were again in short supply. Ernie was dropped for the Liverpool game at Anfield in November 1970, as Brian Hill was brought in to stiffen the team, a 0-0 draw serving to justify Cantwell's change of tactics.

Ernie was in and out of the side until the beginning of April 1971, when he struck a purple patch, enjoying an extended run in midfield until the end of the season. At Easter Manchester United were the visitors to Highfield Road. After five minutes Alex Stepney failed to deal cleanly with a cross from Dave Clements and Ernie, ever the opportunist, pounced on Nobby Stiles' attempted clearance which hit Willie Carr, and crisply drove home from fifteen yards. The goal broke a barren spell of 515 minutes since the Sky Blues last scored and the relief around the ground was palpable. The same pattern was established within four minutes of the second half, when Ernie hit a goal of exquisite power and grace from nothing – a volley from the edge of the box that Stepney watched helplessly as it flashed past him. The crowd were treated to a vintage performance from George Best, who conjured a goal for United but, even though the Irishman's genius dominated the second half, City survived in a determined, courageous performance, with Chris Cattlin and Jeff Blockley excelling in defence. Four days later Ernie was again twice on the scoresheet in the 3-0 home victory over Burnley. With luck Burnley might have reversed the score but, just when they were asserting themselves, Ernie cheekily surprised them with an impudent finish. Collecting the ball a few feet inside the Burnley half, he spotted 'keeper Tony Waiters on the edge of his box. Ernie coolly curled a forty-yard lob reminiscent of David Beckham's goal against Wimbledon, which Waiters desperately managed to get a hand to, but failed to prevent the ball bouncing into an empty net. Four minutes from time Ernie supplied the cross for Billy Rafferty to score his first senior goal at the second attempt. In the dying seconds Willie Carr burst clear from the halfway line and, with the Burnley defence exposed, Ernie screamed for the ball in an unmarked position. Carr crossed perfectly and Ernie unleashed an explosive shot for number three. The defeat all but consigned Burnley to relegation. Derek Henderson in the *Coventry Evening Telegraph* was fulsome in his praise: 'It wasn't long ago that Hunt could not win his place in the City side. Now I think he has proved beyond a shadow of doubt that he has a place – as a potential goal-snatcher played in a middle position. His roles as a midfield player or a man played out wide are clearly not as effective. It was thanks to Hunt that the game sprang to life... Few British footballers would have either read the situation or tried what Hunt did.' Noel Cantwell said afterwards, 'I certainly hadn't noticed where Waiters was, but Ernie can size up these situations. Few people would have even attempted a shot from there.'

Tony Waiters later came to Coventry as coach and at training I used to take the piss out of him – 'Don't come too far off your line, Tony!' I used to enjoy my training apart from the dreaded cross-country runs around Stoneleigh. There were thirty-eight on the run and every time it would be Roy Barry, Maurice Setters and me – thirty-sixth, thirty-seventh and thirty-eighth! Roy and I were given some purple hearts to give us a lift before the start of one season. We were going to save them for the match but pre-season got so tough I had to use them to keep me going. I still finished last in the runs!

The players were weighed by Norman Pilgrim every Monday morning before training in the cafeteria. They wore slips to avoid the embarrassment of any ladies present, but not Ernie the exhibitionist – he would enter stark naked. As he stood on the scales he covered himself with his hands and Pilgrim never realised he was simply using them to press down on the scales to keep his weight down!

Ernie signed off the season at the beginning of May with a fine opportunist goal in the 2-0 home victory over Newcastle United. City were awarded a corner on the right after thirty-six minutes, which was partially cleared. Jim Smith steered it back towards his own penalty area, where Brian Alderson found Chris Cattlin. With the defence pushing up, Cattlin cleverly lifted it over their heads and Ernie blasted the ball first-time high into the net with his customary aplomb. Jeff Blockley confirmed victory with a close range header on sixty-six minutes. City finished just above midway in the table and, while it was felt by some critics that Ernie's free role was something of a luxury when points were in short supply, his goals-for column was indisputable, top-scoring for the second time in three seasons, with 12 goals in 36 appearances. Two days later City left for a tour of Tunisia. Ernie has no recollection of his visit to North Africa – it must have been a cracking trip!

Ten

More Match-Rigging Allegations
1971-1972

By the early 1970s, Ernie's looks had blended with the fashion of the day. With his swarthy appearance, droopy moustache and bow-legged gait, he looked as if he had just strolled onto the pitch from a wild-west scene, or perhaps in keeping with his extraordinary life, maybe a saloon bar. The fastest shot in the West was still delivering the goods.

The 1971/72 season opened with a 'picture goal from the maestro' in the 1-1 home draw against Stoke. Dennis Mortimer sped along the right flank, drew Alan Bloor out of position and flashed across a low centre. Ernie took off with a horizontal header that sent the ball home at the near post with Gordon Banks stranded at the other end of the goal. Stoke's heightened tempo after the break brought parity with an early response from John Ritchie.

In August 1971 City took on West Brom at the Hawthorns. In a tight match it required a goal of stunning execution to unlock the Albion defence. In the fifty-seventh minute Willie Carr, as busy as ever way out on the left flank, angled a perfectly judged forty-five-yard diagonal ball across the Albion back line. It dipped into the right-hand edge of the penalty area and Ernie thundered along the byline to meet it brilliantly first time with an unanswerable volley. It crashed into the roof of the net, giving Jim Cumbes no chance. Tony Brown pounced onto the otherwise faultless Chris Cattlin's back-header to equalize eight minutes later. Eighteen-year-old Mick McGuire made an assured debut in a pulsating local derby.

One of the best goals I scored was the volley against West Brom. Willie played a brilliant ball to me on the edge of the box. I sneaked behind the full-back and hit a volley, it was more luck than judgement, but I hit it really cleanly.

In September 1971 Chelsea's six-game winning run against City ended in a goal-crazy first half. The opposition reckoned without the tigerish Ernie, bruised by the belligerent Chelsea defenders, as he stage-managed the drama. He was an irrepressible force, fashioning all three City goals with a battery of skills. After four

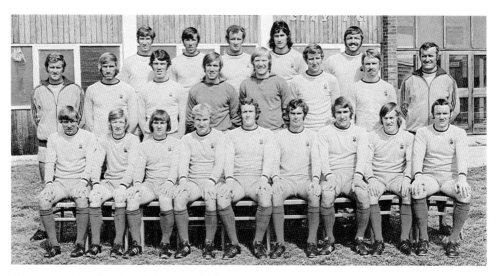

Coventry City 1971/72. From left to right, back row: Strong, Coop, Hill, Mortimer, Hunt. Middle row: Asprey (Coach), Joicey, Rafferty, Glazier, McManus, Cattlin, Parker, Cantwell (Manager). Front row: Machin, Carr, Young, Clements, Blockley, O'Rourke, Smith, Alderson, Barry.

minutes he delivered a perfectly flighted cross from the left on to Billy Rafferty's head for the first. In the fortieth minute he was fouled by David Webb and seized a quick free-kick opportunity to deliver the ball into the Chelsea box. John O'Rourke's explosive power held off Webb's challenge to slice the ball at a narrow angle into the net. Two minutes later Ernie shrewdly rifled a through ball into the path of the lurking Dennis Mortimer, who had crept up from the back four. His fifteen-yard drive caught the Chelsea defence leaden-footed and 'keeper John Phillips could do nothing to prevent Mortimer's firm shot racing past him for his first League goal. Thinking twice as fast as anyone else, Ernie constantly pulled the befuddled Chelsea defence out of position, but goals from Peter Osgood (two) and John Hollins achieved parity for the home side by half-time. Both defences tightened up after the break as the eventful match finished 3-3.

Later the same month it was left to wily Ernie to inject some life into the Coventry attack at home to Nottingham Forest. After three minutes young Bobby Parker picked the ball up just inside the Forest half and found the overlapping Wilf Smith. Smith took the ball down the line and arrowed a cross towards Ernie in the middle. 'keeper Jim Barron was caught in two minds as Ernie met the ball with his head to power it into the net for his 150th League goal. City pressed the fast-forward button as Forest manned the barricades, but fell to a sucker punch when Peter Cormack forced an equalizer midway through the second half.

A 3-1 victory over Leeds at Highfield Road in October 1971 was described by Derek Henderson in the *Evening Telegraph* as, 'The Sky Blues' best result since

First Division football arrived in Coventry just over four years ago.' Nobody thought quicker or more shrewdly than the young veteran Ernie, who was the Man of the Match, followed closely by Quinton Young, who gave Terry Cooper a torrid afternoon. City enjoyed the best possible start in the fifth minute, when Ernie cleverly stepped over a ball from Ian St John to allow it to run on to Chris Chilton who, unmarked, scored from short range – his first goal for the club. Then Ernie breasted down a neat ball for St. John to finish and deservedly scored the third himself ten minutes after the break with a cleverly measured twenty-five-yard chip over Gary Sprake. Two minutes from time a shot by Johnny Giles was deflected into the net by Bobby Parker.

Glazier; Coop, Barry; Smith, Blockley, Parker; Young, Carr, Chilton, Hunt, St John. Sub: Mortimer.

Ernie was still a force when employed to his best advantage and relished the role he had always wanted. He reached peak form that season and was rated one of the best poachers in Britain, with his own brand of shooting skills. Yet the previous season Coventry were prepared to sell him as he vanished into the reserves. Noel Cantwell revealed the need for cash drove him to the brink of selling Ernie – 'But the way he is playing now money just couldn't buy him.' said Cantwell. 'Ernie is doing a great job. He has become one of the most consistent scorers in the League.'

I hadn't been happy playing in midfield and had to ask the boss again for the chance to operate in a free role. I was always confident I could get goals and think I proved my point, as I had twice been the club's leading scorer. Playing in a free role gave me more freedom and the chance to lose defenders. It was tough attacking from the middle because you were always marked tightly and got few scoring chances, but I was getting tremendous help from the rest of the team. Willie Carr could do most things with the ball and was buzzing like a true Scottish international, while the link-up of Ian St John and Wilf Smith brought composure in midfield. We needed the experience and luck to beat Spurs, Everton and Leeds, which showed we were confident of taking on the best. The displays also got the crowd behind us again, it was great to hear them and helped lift the lads.

At the beginning of November 1971, Ernie led the line at home to Huddersfield in place of the injured Chris Chilton and sank the opposition with two fine efforts. Once again the deadly duo of Ernie and Willie Carr dictated the tempo with their invention and craft. On the stroke of half-time Carr's corner swung into the near post where Ernie popped up to glance it into the net from close range. He conjured the second out of nothing in the fifty-first minute. Carr made ground with an unimpeded run on the right and crossed knee-high to the near post. Ernie put a vital half-stride in front of his shadowing defender to hurl himself forward and execute a stunning diving header into the corner of the net. Despite a stirring comeback and a goal through Dave Smith, it was City who finished the afternoon in the ascendancy. One blot on the victory was the gate of 16,400, the lowest at Highfield Road since April 1963. Virtuoso Ernie, in his first game back after an ankle injury, underlined that, whatever his limitations in certain aspects of his play, his sense of an opening near goal was a very precious commodity. Ernie said at the time:

I wasn't worried about getting up to the high balls – I used my extra-long studs, they made me 5 foot 9 inches! I knew there were only seconds left before half-time when I fetched the ball from behind the goal for our corner. No-one marked me and I signalled to Willie. He centred a peach of a ball and I headed in, then he made my second goal with another brilliant pass.

Ernie's superb season was interrupted during a rain-lashed afternoon on 20 November, when he was sent off in the 2-0 home defeat to Liverpool for putting into one succinct phrase what 20,000 other people were probably thinking. He simply summed up Coventry's thoughts on the last twenty minutes which brought a booking for Jeff Blockley and two goals for Jack Whitham, one of which a linesman said was offside. Ernie expressed his feelings to referee Tom Reynolds, standing in for the injured George Hartley, who was in no mood to be charitable. As Noel Cantwell said afterwards, 'Ernie is not a dirty player, he is simply a human being. And what he did was a natural reaction after all the frustration the team had suffered. I know and he knows that he shouldn't have said it.' Ernie was given his marching orders following Liverpool's second goal after eighty-nine minutes. He had continued to argue with Reynolds over his refusal to award a penalty two minutes earlier when Quinton Young had bitten the dust. Ernie was suspended for three weeks and fined £80 for the first punishable offence of his thirteen-year career. He did not seek a personal hearing and was told of the sentence by letter – he said at the time:

There appears to be one set of rules for some and another set for others. The disciplinary committee made such a song and dance about players with bad records, but after this sentence I'm entitled to ask whether having a good record means anything. It sickens me to think the game has come to this. To say I'm choked is putting it mildly. The sentence is unbelievable – when I read the letter I just went numb. I have been booked only three times in thirteen years of football and these were for technical infringements. I am not a kicker and I've never been booked for a violent foul. Now for one lapse in the last minute of a game I get three weeks and a heavy fine. I admit I was in the wrong, I swore at the referee in the heat of the moment. But I was hoping my previous good record would see me through this and at worst I expected a suspended sentence. I shall lose three weeks wages on top of the fine, so the people of Coventry will hear me carol-singing earlier this year!

From early November until April 1972, City managed only one win in nineteen games, a period during which Ernie found it difficult to get back into the side after his suspension. He did make the bench for the FA Cup third round tie at West Brom in January 1972.

When Swindon were promoted to the Second Division everybody got a watch as a reward. For one game I was just going out of the dressing room when I realised I'd still got my watch on. I came back in, took it off and scored a couple of goals. So I did the same thing right up to when I was playing for Coventry. When we played West Brom in the cup, Chris Chilton put us 2-1 up after eighty-one minutes. Near the end Ian St John got injured and came off. I was told to get hold of the ball and waste time in the corner. I forgot I had left my watch on, ran on to the pitch and shouted to the ref, 'Come on ref, it's nearly time.' He looked at his watch and said, 'No it's not.' I said, 'Yes it is, there's two minutes to go, look,' and showed him my watch! He sent me off to remove it which wasted more time and when I came back he blew his whistle.

Ernie was recalled to start the fourth round tie against Hull City in February 1972, having warmed up with a hat-trick for the reserves. An alternative preparation enjoyed by the whole squad was a visit to the Droitwich brine baths. It was all to no avail, as the Sky Blues slumped to a poor 1-0 defeat at the hands of the Tigers, Ernie having a goal disallowed when the referee failed to allow advantage after Wilf Smith was fouled.

With City again in the midst of a relegation battle, the cup defeat was a bitter pill to swallow and Noel Cantwell was dismissed in March 1972. Bob Dennison, the chief scout, was appointed caretaker manager until the end of the season. After a faltering start by Dennison, Ernie scored two priceless goals as City won their first match in twelve in April 1972 by thrashing Everton 4-1, the second match allegedly rigged by Ernie. Both sides had gone eleven games without a win before this crucial evening fixture.

In the twenty-second minute Mike Lyons (not one of those allegedly involved) handled the ball as he challenged Jeff Blockley in the air from a Willie Carr corner. Ernie managed to slide his spot kick under Gordon West. City kept raiding and Willie Carr volleyed home a stunning shot after two minutes of frenzied attacking in the thirty-sixth minute. Lyons miskicked a clearance in midfield from Roy Barry to let Ernie in, who coolly took the ball on and steered it past the oncoming West for the third after forty-three minutes. Coventry made it four for the first time that season seven minutes after the interval. Dennis Mortimer side-footed a free-kick to Ernie, who rattled the bar with a fierce drive. With West groping for the rebound, Chris Chilton headed it home. Everton secured a consolation goal three minutes from time with a David Johnson tap-in. The visitors were described as, 'Looking an incredibly pale facsimile of the side that won the League Championship two seasons ago… lucky to escape with a three-goal margin.'

We were in danger of going down again and I fixed this game for the same millionaire. I approached four Everton players and three of them agreed to 'chuck' the game for £1,000 each. I scored twice and we won 4-1. He gave me £350 and never approached me again. I was very nervous about it, knowing what happened to the Swindon players all those years ago. It was a big thing for me, but I wanted us to stay in the First Division and did it to save Coventry going down – it was not for money. I know it was wrong and I'm not proud of what I did, but I almost convinced myself I was doing it on behalf of Coventry City.

Ernie receives the Player of the Year award for the 1971/72 season from Joe Mercer (left), watched by supporters club chairman Alf Surrey and secretary Jim Wrigley.

1972 – Ernie's sports shop at Keresley. In the picture are Harold Smith, business director, Nigel Chapman, shop manager and Ernie, 'director in charge of buying'.

Ernie finished top scorer for the third time at Coventry with 12 goals in 30 appearances, an achievement that led to him receiving the inaugural award of the Sky Blues' Player of the Year. Another tour was beckoning:

During the summer we went to the Far East, starting in South Korea. Naturally we had a few drinks on the plane and when we landed in Seoul a bloke called Mr Kim came up to me and said, 'You like ladies?' 'Yes, I like ladies very much.' Some of us ended up in a brothel at a time when there was a curfew in force between midnight and 5 a.m. because of the political situation. It was 11.55 p.m. and we were having such a good time we didn't realise what the time was! We got in a taxi which went completely the wrong way back to the hotel with a couple of girls, who asked, 'Any more footballers?' 'Yes, fourteen!' We got them into the hotel via a back entrance and hid them in the bathroom. We were playing South Korea the next day and Roy Barry and I called a team meeting, so we could get the rest of the lads to our room. We opened the bathroom door and these two girls came out. I'll leave the rest to your imagination, but the look on the face of the lads was priceless! Of course Bob Dennison and Eddie Plumley knew nothing about it. I also remember throwing a television set out of a window from a room over there, when a young girl took some money from my wallet and didn't want to pay me back!

We moved on to Japan to play a couple of other games, then at the last minute a decision was taken to play Santos in Thailand. It was just as well, as the plane we were scheduled to take out of Tokyo crashed into the hillside

Coventry's summer tour to the Far East 1972. Ernie comes off the waterlogged pitch alongside Alan Dugdale in Nagoya after beating a Japan XI 3-0.

and there were no survivors. As we got off the plane at Bangkok, they were heaping garlands of flowers round my neck, as they'd heard I'd scored a few goals on the tour and they nicknamed me 'White Pele.' I'd been on the piss and came off at half-time knackered in ninety-degree humidity. I suggested Alan Green went on in my place for the experience, he scored and walked off with Pele's shirt, which I was planning to get – same old story! We drew and Pele scored a penalty when Roy Barry ran into him.

Eleven

From Doncaster to Atherstone via Bristol: 1972-1976

In August 1972, under the new managerial partnership of Gordon Milne and Joe Mercer, Ernie was soon into his stride, scoring from a free-kick in a 1-1 draw at Spurs. At five foot eight inches Ernie was tagged one of 'Mercer's midgets.' He followed that with a penalty in the 1-1 draw at home to Southampton, but disaster struck at the beginning of September in a 2-1 win over Stoke. Ernie's lively brio was tempered when he limped off the field after fifty-eight minutes, as Coventry secured their first win of the season, courtesy of two goals from Willie Carr.

I went up to head the ball with Dennis Smith, landed awkwardly and heard my foot go snap. I limped off and x-rays revealed two cracks in the metatarsal bones between the toes and the ankle in the right foot, the third time that line of weakness had been fractured.

While he was sidelined, and following his success as a feature writer when at Wolves, Ernie also wrote a weekly column for the *Birmingham Sports Argus* without the aid of a ghost writer. However he relied on the manager's secretary Jenny Robinson to do the typing, as his writing was barely legible! He also acquired a reputation as the journalists' best friend, not being averse to feeding stories to the press for a few bob. Once fit, Ernie was unable to regain his place in the first team and nearly returned to Swindon in a deal brokered by Town manager Les Allen. A fee was agreed but Ernie decided to pull out because of his business interests – he didn't want at that stage a move from the Midlands.

I came back in the November as sharp as ever, but there was competition in the form of Colin Stein and Tommy Hutchison. I did have a phone call from Johnny Byrne out in Cape Town, who wanted me to play for him in South Africa but, as far as I could make out Coventry turned it down, as they didn't want to lose me. They were happy to send me out on loan to keep me match

November 1972 in Coventry City colours – the hair is lengthening and the
moustache more pronounced.

fit, so I went for a month to Doncaster, who were managed by my old pal Maurice Setters. I was on £80 per week at Coventry, but got £200 per week playing in the Fourth Division at Doncaster, as they gave me a bonus relating to the size of the gate, which went up dramatically.

Ernie joined Rovers on 25 January 1973 and the loan period was subsequently extended for a further month. His first game was in a 1-0 home defeat by Gillingham. In the next match, a 1-0 home win over Torquay, 'Hunt put in some defence-splitting passes against a square Torquay defence, but his efforts were wasted... Kitchen, served brilliantly by Hunt, missed several good chances.' He followed that in February with a seventy-second-minute goal, which salvaged a point for Rovers in a 1-1 draw at home to Workington. It was the best move of the match, initiated by some neat play from Peter Kitchen and Chris Rabjohn, which led to Ernie flicking home the equalizer after Helliwell scored earlier. In a 2-0 victory at Northampton Town at the beginning of March, Ernie created two goals inside nine minutes, scored by Stan Brookes and John Haselden. In five matches during the first month, with Ernie scheming in midfield, he scored once and helped Rovers take six points. Fourth Division football proved an eye-opener for Ernie.

It was very hard physically, the defenders kicked everything that moved. I was lucky, they didn't kick me because I didn't move much! It was better playing competitive football rather than reserve football and I was glad to help out my old mate Maurice. There were some useful players at Doncaster like Archie Irvine, who reminded me a bit of Willie Carr, a livewire midfield player. But if you played in the back four, you could have kept going until you were sixty! I remember playing against my old Wolves teammate Joe Wilson when I was there. Joe used to come on the bus with his accordion, he was a lovely bloke and I came across him playing for Newport County.

Ernie was injured in the 1-1 home draw with Peterborough on 9 March and returned to Coventry on 22 March. In his first game at Highfield Road after he was recalled, Ernie's appearance in the Central League against Wolves in early April was marked by a neat volley when he scored the second goal in a 4-1 win. By the end of the season he was ready for another tour:

I went to Rhodesia during the summer of 1973 – my namesake Roger Hunt went too and Bill Asprey managed the side. We had a good time and met Ian Smith and visited Victoria Falls. One day we went to a game reserve, the woman on the mike in the coach said, 'Now we're going to the Wankie Game Reserve.' I said, 'Where are we going?' Of course she had to repeat it. 'Oh, what's it called?' All the lads were having a really good craic about it, it appealed to my sense of humour.

Ernie returned to the City first team as substitute in August 1973 after almost a year out, in the 1-0 home win over Liverpool. Manager Gordon Milne said at the time, 'Ernie is one of the most skilful players in the game. He was doing so well in the reserves that I felt we could use his experience.' Ernie restored craft and cunning to City's front line with three consecutive appearances, the first in September 1973, a 1-0 home win over Derby. He displayed a lively understanding with Colin Stein, who swept City into the lead after ten minutes with a powerful header from Wilf Smith's cross. Ernie exercised 'keeper Colin Boulton soon after with a crisp volley. Typically he continued to show the enthusiasm of a teenager in the second half and fooled Boulton into losing the ball, then nearly scoring with an outrageous back-heel flick. He clearly enjoyed his return to the big time and carried that form into a 2-2 draw at Highfield Road against Newcastle four days later.

A mini-resurgence in his Coventry career was, however, short-lived and Ernie's final game in a Sky Blue shirt was on 29 September in a 2-0 win at

During the summer of 1973 Ernie toured Rhodesia. His namesake Roger Hunt is second left and Bill Asprey, who managed the side, is second from the right. Ernie is photographed fifth from the left, immediately next to Premier Ian Smith.

Leicester. It was not a happy farewell as he limped off at half-time with a pulled hamstring, after City went into the lead courtesy of a goal from Brian Alderson. His replacement, debutant Les Cartwright sealed the victory with a fierce shot deflected past Peter Shilton.

Ernie had performed enterprisingly for six years and entertained the Coventry fans with his skills and personality, seeking out the funny side of the game. Always a crowd favourite, he was more importantly a regular goalscorer in an age of defensive football. For three out of four seasons Ernie was leading scorer, but injuries and a change of management had begun to cut him adrift. Bristol City manager Alan Dicks was well aware of Ernie's capabilities, having been with him at Coventry where he was assistant manager. A move to Bristol rescued Ernie from his internal exile and proved a suitable way of extending his playing career. Ernie went initially to Bristol on a month's loan at the end of 1973. It was an inauspicious start on New Year's Day 1974, as in his first appearance City were defeated 2-0 at home to Orient. He was promptly dropped to the bench for the next game, a goal-less draw with Preston, but returned to score a spectacular goal in a 2-1 defeat at Bolton. In the fourth minute Donnie Gillies threaded a ball through to Trevor Tainton, who hared down the right wing and crossed perfectly to Ernie. Instinctively he swerved a twenty-yard volley into the net with his left foot, a collector's item of a goal which drew prolonged applause from both sets of supporters. With City on the back foot however, Bolton responded with an unfortunate own goal from Geoff Merrick and the winner from Roy Greaves.

When I went on loan to Bristol, I thought I had played my last game at Bolton. I hit a volley with my left foot from Trevor's cross into the top corner and it rocketed into the net. I only used my left peg for standing on and I think that persuaded Alan Dicks to sign me the next week. I liked the set-up at Bristol, they were the best group of youngsters I'd played alongside since my Swindon days and I thought I could do a job for them. I had a specific role to play, on the right side of midfield, drifting wide and inside, and stopping the left-back coming through. The young lads were full of running and effort, but sometimes they were a bit over-eager. There were times when you needed to slow a game down and that was the job I was brought in to do.

Alan Dicks signed the thirty-year-old permanently for £7,000 on 25 January 1974. Dicks saw Ernie's experience as the ideal replacement for Bobby Gould, who had been transferred to West Ham. Frank O'Farrell also made a strong bid for Ernie to join Cardiff City and Swindon would have loved to welcome their old hero back into the fold.

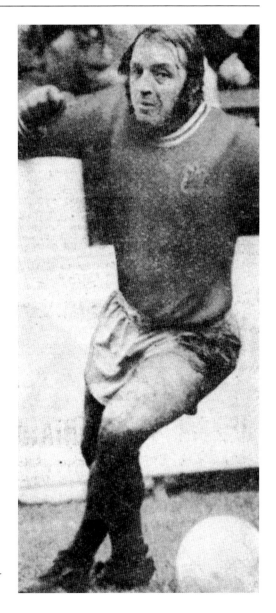

February 1974 – a determined Ernie in action for
Bristol City.

In February 1974 Ernie astounded his old foes West Bromwich Albion at The
Hawthorns with a legal variation of the 'donkey' free-kick. City were awarded a
free-kick in the fifteenth minute just outside the penalty area when Keith Fear
was tackled from behind by Alistair Robertson. Ernie, conducting operations,
stood legs astride the ball as six Albion men lined up in the defensive wall, with
three City men jostling alongside to add to the confusion. Tiptoeing behind,
Donnie Gillies put his toe through Ernie's legs and scooped the ball knee high.
Ernie took it on the volley and the ball flew past astonished 'keeper Peter

Latchford on its inexorable route to goal. John Wile headed an equalizer for the Baggies four minutes later, but City again took the lead ten minutes after the interval, when Ernie curled in a free-kick which Trevor Tainton turned past Latchford. City were denied victory when Jeff Astle levelled with a late goal.

The West Brom goal was a one-off, it was known as the 'Nutcracker' or the 'Sillett Special,' as it was our coach John Sillett's idea. We'd been practising free-kicks in training, but it's the first time we tried it in a match. It could be a bit painful if Donnie miskicked! John went through the various free-kicks and numbered them one to eight, which was the Nutcracker. Then he put me in charge, I told him I didn't go to university and it would take me all night to remember that lot!

In the FA Cup Ernie was prominent in a hard-earned victory over Hereford United in the fourth round, hours after signing a permanent deal to join City. Here was a throbbing encounter precariously balanced on an extended tightrope from first to last, and played on a pitch more suitable for planting rice than playing football. In the seventeenth minute Ernie appeared to pull Ronnie Radford's shirt, but the referee gave a free-kick in City's favour. Ernie wasted no time in shrewdly planting a deep cross from close to the corner flag to the near post into the path of Geoff Merrick, who cleverly glanced the ball with his trusty left foot into the far corner of the net past Tommy Hughes. Man of the Match Ernie personified domestic cup football at it's best – he was the only player to refuse a change of kit at half-time although dripping with mud from head to toe, and controlled the middle of a waterlogged park. John Sillett purred, 'He's earned his transfer fee already,' before he knew City's opponents in the next round were mighty Leeds United, the undefeated First Division leaders.

With an average age of twenty-three and seven local players, it was vital that City were able to draw on the veteran's wisdom, but Ernie nearly didn't make it as he struggled with fluid on the knee. Passing a late fitness test, he was prominent in calming the nerves of the younger players. As captain Geoff Merrick was geeing everyone up in the dressing room, he turned to Ernie and said, 'Tell us a joke Ernie.' His joke book came out, he delivered and everyone ran out laughing. Leeds couldn't fathom out what was happening and in a way never recovered. In front of 37,111 passionate supporters, City's 'inferior' squad tore up the script to force a replay at Elland Road. Towards the end of the first half Keith Fear shot on the turn from the edge of the penalty area with his left foot and saw the ball cannon off David Harvey's hand and thud against the bar. Leeds' response was instant. Just before half-time Billy Bremner scored with a beautifully clean strike from twenty-five yards out. In the sixty-fifth minute Gerry Gow played a ball to the edge of the area and, with the defence caught square, Fear controlled the ball deftly and slotted home the equalizer with a delicate lob as Harvey left his line. As City pushed forward for the winner Fear crossed to Ernie, who nodded the ball to Donnie Gillies. City's Scottish striker headed powerfully but Harvey, who kept Leeds in the game, touched the ball over the bar from point-blank range.

The burring busload set off for the hills of Yorkshire in confident mood for the replay. Again Ernie was in doubt until the last minute with an ankle injury, but in an inspired performance City secured victory in front of 47,182 spectators. The only goal came in the seventy-third minute with a superbly worked move. Gerry Gow linked up with Keith Fear, who found Donnie Gillies on the edge of the box. Evading a challenge from Norman Hunter, Gillies showed power and acceleration, and his left-foot shot crept inside the post to Harvey's right-hand side. In a pulsating final fifteen minutes Leeds corralled City into a defensive pen. Bryan Drysdale headed off the line from Joe Jordan in the eighty-second minute with Ray Cashley beaten and a minute later Cashley managed to tip a header from Allan Clarke over the bar. It was a victory earned the hard way through a magnificent team effort. City were the better side on the day, fought for every ball and gave Leeds no breathing space. It was labelled their finest performance in the cup since the Second World War, exemplified by the inspired Gerry Gow, as he outran and outfought Billy Bremner, who generously acknowledged, 'He worked like a boatload of navvies.'

Cashley; Sweeney, Drysdale; Gow, Collier, Merrick; Tainton, Ritchie, Fear, Gillies, Hunt. Sub: Rodgers.

If any reminder of Ernie's pedigree and influence was required, it came in spades from the little man, who moved sweetly and knotted City's midfield into a formidable unit. He rated the ties as two of the best team performances he had ever taken part in – quite a claim from a man with over 500 senior appearances to his credit. With his carefully coiffured hair now starting to recede, one paper described him as 'strutting through the midfield like a balding Chicago cop'.

I remember we were hanging on in the replay with about five minutes left and Bryan Drysdale was struggling. I was trying to stop the game and when I challenged big Joe Jordan, I fell back holding my head. I said to Jack Taylor, the ref, 'Look, ref, he's kicked me in the head, my tooth's stuck in the back of my mouth.' But Jack wasn't having any of it – he probably remembered I had a false tooth and said, 'You always were ugly!' I was trying to prevent Peter Lorimer taking his usual raking type of corner. Lorimer kept waving me back

February 1974 – A memorable moment for Ernie, as he receives the Second Division Player of the Month award from City manager Alan Dicks, a gallon of whisky. In the background are his teammates Gerry Gow, Donnie Gillies, David Rodgers and Ray Cashley.

and when Jack came up and told me to get back, I told him we'd gone metric. Jack was alright, he was one of the refs you could have a laugh and joke with. Afterwards the Leeds players were as good as gold. I remember Paul Madeley came up and wished me well and said we deserved to win.

In recognition of his contribution to the side's success, Ernie won the Second Division Player of the Month award for February 1974 – a gallon of whisky!

In reaching the sixth round for the first time in fifty-four years, City enjoyed another plum tie, this time at home to Liverpool in March 1974. It was billed as City's biggest game for more than fifty years. The omens were not promising when young skipper Geoff Merrick, who had injured his ankle gardening, failed a fitness test on the morning of the match, leaving Ernie to captain the side. While David Rodgers played soundly against John Toshack, Merrick's driving influence was missed. City seldom managed to get behind Liverpool's experienced defence, but they did create half-chances. A first-half drive from Gerry Sweeney, who played Steve Heighway out of the game, went just wide and when Ernie passed to Keith Fear, he shot straight at Ray Clemence from twenty-five yards. In the best City move of the game, Clemence dived on a half-hit shot from Trevor Tainton and Gillies pushed the ball into the net, but was fractionally offside. A messy goal three minutes into the second half came at the wrong psychological time for the young City side. Twice Gary Collier almost stopped Kevin Keegan's run down the left before Bryan Drysdale's headed clearance hit Toshack. The ball bounced down perfectly for Toshack to finish clinically and the goal seemed to lift a boulder off Liverpool's back. Perhaps a draw might have been a fairer result in front of a crowd of 37,671. Danny Blanchflower reported in the *Sunday Express*, 'Ernie Hunt tried to give City direction, but the Liverpool goal destroyed their plans.' Ernie was replaced by John Emmanuel with nineteen minutes left in a tactical change designed to inject more pace out wide.

It was disappointing to lose, as it was the nearest I ever got to Wembley. I never had a decent cup run with my other clubs and it would have been nice to have played at Wembley. It is every player's dream and would have made up for the disappointment of not getting selected for England Schoolboys or not playing there with the England Under-23s.

Although Ernie played in the 1-0 home defeat to Aston Villa the week after the Liverpool game, he was troubled by a persistent knee injury. City's best chances against Villa stemmed from Ernie, his old skills bursting through as he shrugged off John Gidman and Pat McMahon to turn the ball inside, but Keith Fear was unable to capitalize. The 'Nutcracker' free-kick was again attempted, but came to nothing as it thudded into the chest of Ian Ross, standing no more than five yards away. City's unspectacular form in the League could not be camouflaged by the cup run, as they suffered a hangover for the remainder of the season, languishing at sixteenth place in the Second Division. Injury restricted Ernie to 9 League appearances, plus 2 as sub. A summer tour of Greece lightened the mood considerably in the camp:

Bryan Drysdale, who we used to call 'Speedy', and I went out one night. We got a bit loose and ended up singing karaoke at some holiday camp over there. At the end of the evening we broke into their restaurant, but the only thing we could find to eat was a load of chocolate ice cream in one of the freezers. When we got back to the hotel my room-mate Gerry Gow, who'd also

March 1974 –
Ernie is out-jumped
by Tommy Smith in
the FA Cup defeat
by Liverpool.

been out drinking, was dead to the world on the bed, so we smeared this ice cream over certain parts of his body, and when he woke up in the morning he thought he'd **** himself! He went barmy with me but fortunately he had a sense of humour as well. I denied having anything to do with it.

We all went down on the beach one day and the lads, who all knew I couldn't swim, helped me get to this floating raft a couple of hundred yards out. We got on the raft and they all disappeared for about three hours before I was rescued. I think that was probably Gerry's idea, that's why I got my own back.

135

In the summer of 1974 Bristol City toured Greece, where Ernie and Bryan Drysdale exercised their vocal chords.

After one appearance as substitute at Oldham in August 1974, Ernie was released by City in November 1974. In the autumn of his career he joined Atherstone Town, struggling just off the foot of the table in the Premier Division of the Southern League and managed by Gil Merrick, the former Birmingham and England goalkeeper. Playing again in midfield, Ernie's first game was a victory in the Floodlit Cup against Alfreton. He made his home debut at Sheppy Road in a League fixture against Dover and did not disappoint the expectant crowd of 612, a fifty per cent increase on the normal gate. Atherstone struggled to make any real impression on a young Dover side until the eightieth minute, when Ernie latched onto a pass from Bobby Mellor. From about twelve yards out he connected with his left foot and the ball rocketed into the net to give Hughes, the custodian, no chance. Town's jubilation was short-lived as Dover equalized four minutes later through Wallace. Shortly before the end the superb reflexes of Atherstone 'keeper Colin Withers robbed Dover of the winner. He finger-tipped over the bar a stinging free-kick from Arnold on the edge of the box. A hard-earned point and Ernie was on his way to help Atherstone finish the season in mid-table.

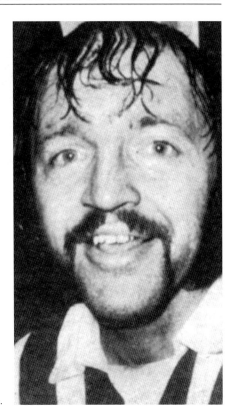

1974 – Ernie in Atherstone Town colours.

When I was released by Bristol City I could have gone to Northampton, but I'd lost my driving licence again and was offered a job playing at Atherstone, where I could get to from Coventry. I took a young lad under my wing, who used to drive me there. I looked after him, he was a good little player but he never made it. He was a lovely Brummie lad, who I think went to play in America. We were driving home once after training, I was driving but shouldn't have been, when a police car drove in front of us. I dived out of the driving seat into the passenger seat and swapped with this lad. Inevitably I'd had a few drinks and one of the policeman, who knew who I was, said I was driving. I asked politely if they could prove it. We had to go to court but they couldn't prove it. Years later the police brought a team down to Ledbury to play the local cricket team and came into my pub afterwards. One of the coppers said to me, 'Do you remember that time when you got away with that drink-driving?' He came down especially to have a go at me. I wasn't that bad, but probably shouldn't have been driving.

I got a bad knock with Atherstone towards the end of my career when a 'keeper came smacking into me and split my head open. With blood pouring down my face you couldn't see the colour of my jersey, it was so red. I was waiting for the ambulance in the dressing room when Gil came in at half-time and said, 'Are you all right for the second half, Ern?' And he meant it! I've got the scar to show on my forehead, but I was lucky really as I never had a bad injury. I was never afraid of goalkeepers and if I felt I had a chance of scoring I'd be in there. I did used to be wary of Reg Matthews of Coventry and Derby, as every time I went into the area to head the ball he would come and smack two bales out of me. Sam Burton used to be like that as well, he even did it to his own players during a game if they got in the way.

Ernie's last appearance was predictably unorthodox. Atherstone had enjoyed a highly successful 1975/76 season and at the end of the campaign travelled to Yeovil, needing a win to finish second to Wimbledon, who were heading for the Football League. Ernie had been injured for the last month, but watched his teammates lose the match as Yeovil clinched the runners-up spot. After the game, the players and officials went to a local restaurant to celebrate the excellent season they had enjoyed. Midway through the evening Ernie disappeared into the kitchen and eventually emerged wearing a maid's apron... and nothing else. His assets were evident for all to see! The rest of his body was staring to betray Ernie and the old warhorse bade farewell to football in May 1976 at the age of thirty-three, with an overall tally of 165 goals to his name in 467 League appearances.

One winter night we were playing at Corby in freezing conditions. It was sleeting and there were about forty people watching. I looked round at Malcolm Beard and said, 'What the hell are we doing here!' We both laughed and carried on with the game, but I knew it was time and I retired at the end of the season. I enjoyed it at Atherstone, there were a lot of ex-pros there who just wanted to carry on playing as long as they could, as they loved the game. We had Colin Withers from Aston Villa, who I used to share a pint of gin with after matches, Joe Kiernan from Northampton and Johnny Vincent and Malcolm from Birmingham City, so it wasn't a bad side. Gil Merrick of course played in goal for England in the famous 6-3 defeat against Hungary at Wembley in 1953. One day at training he was standing by the side of the goal and put up his hand to stop a ball. He missed it and someone shouted out '7-3!'

Atherstone was my last club, I knew it was time to pack in when the linesman started overtaking me! I'd had a good time, but there were other priorities, like the family. I carried on playing occasional charity football and one of the last games I remember was at Leamington, when Jasper Carrott and Stanley Matthews also played.

1975 – Ernie in action for Atherstone Town.

Ernie reflected on a long and rewarding career:

I like to think I played consistently well over a number of years and there wasn't one season in particular which I look back on as my best. People think I'm as soft as shit, as I help them all over the place, but on the pitch I was very competitive. I would never have got as far as I did just with natural talent, it had to be combined with that level of aggression and determination, without being nasty.

It would be unfair to the other players to highlight one particular striker I worked well with, but Neil Martin was probably the best I played with. I scored quite a few goals with the way he held the ball up and knocked it down to me. Having said that, I always seemed to get on with Hugh McIlmoyle, although I didn't play for a long time with him. He used to run at people and we seemed to click with his knock-downs, in a similar way to Jack Smith in the early days at Swindon. Joe Royle at Everton would have been ideal for me, but Harry Catterick played me out of position on the wing, which was very frustrating. When I saw Peter Chamberlain, who was with me at Swindon and is an Evertonian, he said he was disappointed as he thought I would do really well there, but it happens in the game.

The hardest opponent I played against from a physical point of view was Cliff Huxford at Southampton. He said, 'I'll stop you playing' and battered two bales of shit out of me! He was a hard bastard, a harder player than Norman Hunter or 'Chopper' Harris. I played for Swindon against him two or three times, but it never bothered me. Cliff's brother Colin was with us at Swindon for a while. I told him to tell his brother to stop giving me stick or I'd shoot him! Two others were Mike Thresher, a left-back and Tommy Casey, a left half, both with Bristol City. They'd kick their grandmothers given half a chance, but off the pitch they were as nice as pie.

With a reputation for unleashing some shuddering challenges, Cliff Huxford recalls those battles: 'I remember Ernie wasn't that tall, he was quite stocky and a useful player. It was my job as a defender to pick the opposition danger-man out. As he scored a lot of goals, (manager) Ted Bates would have told me to try and play him out of the game. In those days there was more man-to-man marking than nowadays. People tell me I had a bit of a reputation of being a hard man. Mind you I took a few knocks myself along the way, but you accept it and get on with the game.'

I never used to worry about the opposition, you can't afford to, otherwise it would have affected my game. Technically Bobby Moore was the best I ever played against. I usually had a good game against him but I never scored, he was that type of player who just did his job of stopping you scoring.

I always had a great rapport with supporters. The best atmosphere I ever experienced were the games when Swindon and Wolves got promotion. The only negative incident I can remember was when Coventry played Swindon in the League Cup (October 1968). I passed the ball back to the 'keeper from near the dugout, it went for a corner and all the Swindon fans booed me. Coventry played some defensive football in my time and I felt I had to try and entertain them to liven up things. At Wolves there were disabled people in their wheelchairs and buggies by the touchline and I tried to involve them in the game. Towards the end of one match which we were winning, just to waste a bit of time I went to one of them and said, 'Can you take this throw-in for me?' You can't believe how their faces lit up when I spoke to them, but I had to quickly concentrate again as I was in danger of getting emotional about it. I always seemed to win the fans over, even at Everton.

I was a bit frightened of Bert Head to start with, but he was like a father to me. I learnt a lot from him, as I was just a lad and he gave me a lot of advice, but also knew when to give me a bollocking. He picked me in the first team as a sixteen-year-old and I have the highest regard for him. Danny Williams was a nice bloke! In the end I asked for a transfer at Swindon as I wanted to get on. I had seen Mike Summerbee move on and felt it was time for me to go as well. I had a lot of time for Ronnie Allen and Joe Mercer was an excellent manager and like Bert Head, a father figure. Bob Dennison was a good bloke but too soft. Maurice Setters was a brilliant guy and great fun. With all the managers I played under, I never had one who would throw teacups around the dressing room. They were all pretty calm, although when harsh words had to be said, they didn't hold back.

Noel Cantwell was also a decent bloke and when he got the sack Quinton Young and I said we wouldn't play. He had to cope with Ernie Hannigan, Neil Martin, Ian Gibson, Maurice Setters and myself, who all liked a drink. He sort of turned a blind eye, but he would know and was pretty understanding. I would discipline myself during the week and after Wednesdays I would never have a drink, but made up for it at the weekend. I used to get psyched up for the game, which people didn't really realize, but afterwards if we lost I would be the first up to the bar, likewise if we won. On Tuesdays at training especially I would run my socks off and get it out of my system. Although Waggy and I went out for a drink at Wolves, there wasn't a drinking culture like at Coventry. The only time I drank on a Friday night was when Waggy and I went out sometimes and had a game of dominoes, just to relax.

Twelve
From Pulling Pints to Pushing Ladders: 1974-2004

Bristol City offered me a job looking after the youth team, but I had opened a sports shop in Coventry in about 1973 and felt I had to go back and take a more active role in it. Not being big-headed but they partly came into the shop to see me. I was in partnership with a friend, Harold Smith, he was a local hotelier and we kept the shop until about 1976, when it went bust, as neither of us really was able to devote enough time to it.

Ernie became landlord of the Full Pitcher public house in Ledbury, but losses flowed as freely as complimentary pints of bitter dished out by the benevolent host. Some of his antics at the pub were for reasons best known to his therapist.

I was introduced to the pub trade by Jimmy Lee, who was the left-back at Swindon. I was looking for a pub in Coventry, but they couldn't find one for me. Me owning a pub was like giving a match to an arsonist! I was brought up with a beer in my hand, but disciplined myself not to drink when I was playing football until the weekend, when I would let fly. When the football finished, I started drinking more than ever before, it was all too handy. I was probably an alcoholic by then, as it was there all the time, and it was nothing for me to get through a bottle of vodka a day.

My pub was at the bottom of the road and I vaguely remember having a race with a punter from the Top Cross crossroads to my pub down the High Street late at night. He thought he was quicker than me, but we were about as slow as each other. We had a bet on it, I won by an inch and a half, the only difference was that neither of us had any clothes on! I used to serve behind the bar with an apron on, nothing else, not to attract the female clientele, but to scare the men away!

We had a local bobby at Ledbury called Fred Daniels. Fred would walk in at about 10.30 p.m., just before closing time. I said to the locals, 'When Fred comes in, hold your glass, don't rush to get your drink down.' He used to wear

Above and opposite: 1983 – mine host at the Full Pitcher, Ledbury.

a peaked cap and, if he sat at the bar, turned his cap round and started singing On Top of Old Smokey, *you could drink all night and he'd stay with us until about four in the morning. If he didn't, you knew you couldn't get an extension. I was on the outskirts of the town, it was only a small place and I'm not sure what determined it. Perhaps if he didn't think there was going to be any hassle about, he would come down – he was a smashing bloke.*

My dad loved the outdoor life, he was very much a country-loving man. He often came to the pub and we'd go for a walk over the playing fields. He had bandy legs, one of which was dodgy, just like me now. One day Jason, our Labrador, was on the cricket pitch and picked up what I thought was a ball and put it in his mouth. When we reached him we realized it was a big hand grenade and quickly got him to put it down and walked on. Of course Jason picked it up again and dropped it at our feet. My dad said, 'I think it's a live grenade, Roger.' So he hobbled across and gingerly put it right in the middle of the cricket pitch. We got to the back door of the pub and Jason of course had retrieved it again, as Labradors do! I threw it right in the middle of the cricket pitch again and phoned the police. Eventually two of them came down and tiptoed across the cricket field. When they got ten yards away, I heard one of them say, 'What will we do?' 'Go and put your helmet on the grenade,' said the

other one. He didn't fancy that at all and told his mate in no uncertain terms what he could do with his helmet. Eventually one of them did place his helmet over the grenade and they crept back to the pub – it was hilarious. They called for assistance and the SAS turned up from Hereford! They stuffed it in a cushioned container in the boot of a car and shot off at about fifty miles an hour over the uneven pitch. I've never seen anything like it and we eventually found out it was a live grenade. Apparently the back of my pub had been used as a munitions store in the war.

I organised a trip to Birmingham with my customers once to see my old mate Freddie Starr. He supports Everton and that's how I got to know him. I used to watch him at a nightclub on Merseyside before he became famous. I went to see him before the show and told him I was sitting next to a girl with big tits. He gave me an Elvis Presley wig so he knew exactly where I would be. During the show he went into the audience and looked at the girl next to me. 'There's a couple of nice one's here,' he said as he looked at her low-cut dress. He turned to me: 'What about you mate?' He whipped the wig off my head and exclaimed, 'Bloody hell, you're bald!' I looked embarrassed and of course the audience knew nothing about what had gone on beforehand and went wild. It was a great night. I used to pick Freddie up, as he went training with us at Coventry. For a footballer he was a great comedian – how can you play in Wellingtons and a German outfit? He was a nightmare. I used to panic like mad when he was about, as I never knew what he was going to do next. When Coventry got beaten at Manchester City once, he came into the dressing room and said to me, 'Ernie you were crap.' I thought he was going to say what a good game I'd had.

Fred West, the notorious murderer, used to play darts sometimes in the pub. One day he asked if I wanted any building work done. I'm glad I declined! It was a lovely pub, with cricket, football and rugby pitches out the back and I got together a pub team. I even played rugby for Ledbury Town once, when they were one short. I was still 'topped-up' from the night before. They put me out on the wing, but I got bored and came inside. I still only touched the ball once, but ended up with eight stitches in my head and the shirt ripped off my back! 'Well done Ernie,' the coach said, 'Can you play next week?'

Mike Summerbee and Alan Ball came down once to raise a few quid for a local Under-13s school team, so they could buy a minibus, and George Best also came down to raise funds for charity. I enjoyed it, but used to give all the drinks away, the softie that I am, so the pub never made a profit. After nine years I had to come out as I nearly went bankrupt.

Ernie played in the occasional charity match and turned out at Southampton in 1986 for an All-Stars XI against an ex-Bristol City and Rovers XI. It was said that

Ernie is reunited with former lodger and teammate Mike Summerbee at the Full Pitcher after a charity match.

during one testimonial Ernie was revived on the pitch when the stretcher-bearers handed him a gin and tonic:

Not true, it was a vodka and lemonade! If ever I went through a bad patch when I was playing or felt sorry for myself, I went to the Coventry and Warwickshire Hospital and saw the kids with only one leg or whatever. There are always people worse off than yourself and it used to put things into perspective. It would give me a kick up the backside and made me feel better, so in about 1986 I took a job looking after maladjusted children just outside

Ledbury. I still had a drink but, looking after kids, you had to be more responsible, so I was able to cut back on the booze. I found that very rewarding and did it for a couple of years. I regularly took the kids to Goodison for a treat, Howard Kendall would pay for it all, it was a very emotional experience. Then my mum and dad both fell ill, my mum had Parkinson's disease and my dad severe ulcers. I had to pack the job in and moved back to Swindon, where I was closer to my parents and took a job at the County Ground in the commercial department.

Battling against increasing weight, a drink-driving conviction brought that avenue to a thudding halt. It was decided to give Ernie a further period at Swindon to see if he could make a contribution without a car, but the loss of his driving licence led to pressure to sack him. It was a difficult decision for the club to make, as sponsors would invariably make a beeline to Ernie and ignore the commercial manager at the various functions he attended. He then secured a job in the commercial department of Beazer Premier League side Gloucester City as a sales agent in the lottery office and also coached the City youth side.

In November 1989 Ernie made his serious Coventry match-fixing allegations in the Sunday People. The bribes scandal rocked Coventry City and the Football Association considered launching an investigation. Ernie paid the price for his revelations when Gloucester dismissed him for gross misconduct.

Everything I said in the article was the truth, people involved in football know it goes on. I can't name the players involved, but I was chosen because I knew so many players in the game. I went to the Sunday People, *as it was around the time I split up with Anne. I needed money to pay for her mortgage and to help me move to Gloucester, so I could start afresh with Carole, who became my second wife.*

I split from Anne in 1989 because I was a bit of a boy with the women and was still drinking too much. She was worthy of someone better than me and it was hard to start with, but Carole and I got together soon after, which was the best thing that could have happened to me. She has been a great calming influence on me over the years. I had known Carole from my Coventry days, as she is a Coventry girl and saw her before I split up from Anne, I went over the top. I originally met her in 1968 when she ran a dirty-book shop right by Highfield Road – I was her first customer! A smashing bloke called Clive Hall, who had the Wellington Hotel in Gloucester and knew me as he was a Bristol City fan, put me and Carole up for nothing, just to survive when I first split from Anne. He hid us for three months, changing our rooms about and I felt like the Scarlet Pimpernel. On the first night we broke the bed – I didn't jump off the wardrobe!

New Year's Eve 1991 – Ernie
and Carole in role-reversal.

In 1990 Ernie started working full time as a window cleaner in Gloucester. By
the early nineties he had the girth of a Pavarotti and the hairstyle of Max Wall,
but the crack-a-minute slapstick sense of humour continued in the style of Paul
Gascoigne. With his rubber-ball face, Ernie also added the art of gurning to his
extensive repertoire.

Window cleaning was one of the summer jobs I used to do at Swindon with
Cliff Jackson, and I had been doing it on and off for a couple of years with a
lad called Jim, who used to come into the pub at Ledbury. When I worked for
Gloucester City, I got Jim a job there – I'd lost my licence, so he drove me
around. We'd do window cleaning during the day and worked for City selling

149

lottery tickets in the evening. When I left the football club we canvassed for business and got a round in Gloucester, so I moved on to that full time. Carole and I used to go into an ice-cream parlour in Gloucester after cleaning the Debenhams windows nearby, run by an ex-referee who I knew from my playing days – I think it was Harry New. I promoted his shop by cycling on his ice-cream bike round town singing the 'Cornetto' song.

One day in about 1993 I was ten foot up the ladder, it slipped and I fell on my back into a step going into the doorway. It winded me and I ended up on my hands and knees by the front door. Jim looked at me and said, 'Do you want me to phone Carole?' I replied, 'No, f**k that, phone for an ambulance!' The door opened and the lady owner came out and I crawled on my hands and knees into the front room. She phoned for the ambulance and asked me if I wanted a cup of tea. I said I'd prefer a brandy. As I sat in the armchair I moved back and felt the sound of my ribs cracking. They were worried in case I had punctured my lung and must have given me some morphine. They took me to the Gloucester Royal Hospital, x-rayed me and found I had broken eight ribs. I was black with bruises and Carole was on the phone crying her eyes out. I said, 'Don't worry, I'll be all right.' She sobbed, 'I've just lost Roger the budgie,' I thought she was crying for me! I was in hospital for about a week and that put paid to my window cleaning for months. Fortunately Jim carried on with it. He was a smashing lad.

Ernie also suffered hip problems as a legacy of his footballing days and by 1995 had been waiting almost three years for a replacement on the NHS. He was told he couldn't have the operation unless he lost weight – he'd risen to over fifteen stone – but Ernie argued he couldn't lose weight as he couldn't walk. In desperation he rang the Professional Footballers Association.

The hip first started playing up in the early nineties, but they wouldn't do it on the NHS as they said at sixteen stone I was too heavy and too young. I swallowed my pride and phoned Mick McGuire at the PFA, who I was with at Coventry. Within days I was given the go-ahead to book myself in. It cost £5,200 at the Winfield Private Hospital and the PFA paid for £5,000. A director at the hospital was a Coventry supporter and said, 'Don't worry about the £200.' Two days later the operation was carried out by the bloke who said I was too fat and too young. I was beginning to think everyone had forgotten me, but thanks to the PFA I felt like a two-year-old again.

Window cleaning was my last job, I went back to it after my operation, but I stood at the bottom of the ladder, while the young lads would go up it, but I even had to pack that up in the end. I've lost a lot of weight over the last couple of years and feel much better for it. In 2003 I had a second operation on the

1995 – wedding photo of Ernie and Carole. Also in the picture are Symone and her children Jack, Jessica and Clark.

Mid-nineties – Ernie and Carole.

right hip and was back in hospital in 2004 when I cracked my femur. I wasn't trying to recreate the donkey free-kick at the time, I slipped on a wet tile.

In 1996 Ernie was named in the *Coventry Evening Telegraph*'s line-up of twelve Sky Blue legends who represented the elite of the club over the previous thirty seasons. He had long patched up his differences with Coventry City regarding the match-fixing allegations and for a while was involved in corporate hospitality on match days. Cheered on by an encouraging crowd, in July 2002 Ernie and Willie Carr re-enacted the donkey free-kick before a pre-season friendly with Dundee United at Highfield Road.

At the beginning of 2001 I was a guest when Coventry played at Swindon in the FA Cup. Carole's eldest grandson, Clark came onto the pitch with me and this fella stuck a mike up my nose and said, 'Who do you think's going to win, Ernie?' As I had been voted in the programme the best ever player to play for both clubs, I replied diplomatically, 'A draw,' it was the easy way out. Coventry won 2-0 and after the game when I reached the boardroom, Carole and her daughter Symone were break-dancing to the music over the tannoy.

July 2002 – Ernie and Willie Carr attempt to recreate the donkey free-kick before a pre-season friendly against Dundee United. Tucked inside Ernie's shirt is one of his wigs.

The directors and guests were lapping it up, I don't think they'd ever seen anything like that in the boardroom before!

A few years ago Ernie had a book on following the fortunes of Coventry City named after him titled *Ernie Hunt's Sideburns*. In September 2003 he sold the battered Adidas boots with which he scored the donkey free-kick to Ian McLatchie, a lifelong City fan, who placed them on display at the Quadrant Club in Coventry city centre. Proprietor Mark Fleming said, 'It's superb, lots of people have come in just to have a look at the boots. It's a part of history, I was at the match and everyone can remember that goal. Afterwards everyone was doing the donkey free-kick.'

At the end of the season I scored that goal, someone told me to keep the boots because they might be worth something one day, as the free-kick had been banned. I didn't think much of it at the time, but I had been holding on to them to pass on to my grandson and hadn't really thought about selling them. But the offer of £500 was a decent one and I had no problems selling as it meant they will stay in Coventry.

2001 – Ernie salutes the crowd with Clark at the Swindon *v.* Coventry FA Cup tie.

October 2003 – proprietor Mark Fleming shows Ernie and Willie Carr the boots Ernie scored the 'donkey' free-kick with, that are displayed at the Quadrant Club in Coventry.

I have two children from my first marriage, Nicola born in 1970 and Sally-Anne, born in 1973. Nicola, who lives in Ledbury with her boyfriend Saacs, helps look after animals. She must have inherited some of my sporting genes, as she swam for England at Under-16 level and had England Youth trials at hockey. Sally-Anne, who lives in Worcester with her husband Kevin, works part-time in the travel business. Sally-Anne has two children, Bethany and Oliver, who are four and two. Carole and I married in 1995 – Carole has one child, Symone, who has three children: Clark, fifteen, Jessica, who is eleven and Jack, who is nine. It wasn't easy to adapt to life after football, but I've got a lovely family and have no complaints. My hobbies are mainly the family and also helping people. We have lived in rented accommodation at Gloucester since about 1992, we have a great landlord Tony McNulty, but we hope to return soon to Coventry.

Above: Daughter Nicola and boyfriend Saacs.

Left: Daughter Sally-Anne with husband Kevin, with Bethany and Oliver.

Opposite: Carole's daughter Symone, with Jack and Jessica.

Thirteen

I Like Driving in my Car

A quiet life is an anathema to some folk, Ernie included, notably when it comes to his motoring exploits.

My first car was a Vauxhall 37, which I bought when I was about seventeen. I didn't have to take my test, as when I got in the car the examiner said, 'Can you get us a couple of tickets for the match on Saturday?' I said, 'Yes,' so he told me to drive round the corner and passed me! I put my thumbs up to Mike Summerbee, who was waiting to take his test and the bloke got two tickets off him as well. The Vauxhall had the type of indicators that flapped out of the side and I used to hit my head on them as I got out of the car. Then I went upmarket when I was about twenty and bought an A35, which was in the John Boorman film. I kept it until I went to Wolves, when I bought a MGB. I bought a red one, but I didn't know I was going to move to Everton later! As I was only on Merseyside for six months, I held on to it, although I was a bit worried as one of my teammates had his red car trashed.

Then in 1968 I bought an E-type Jag with the two grand I got paid by Coventry for staying in the First Division. It lasted a couple of years until I forgot to put oil in the engine and it packed up. I was hopeless at maintenance, as long as I put petrol in it I thought it was all right. I swapped it for a Sovereign Jaguar and the first time I drove it I went to see Carole. On the way I had to stop as there was an accident in the road. A fella came up to me and said, 'You're Ernie Hunt, aren't you? Have you got any lights?' I looked for the lights and set the windscreen wipers off! Yes, I'd had a drink. I eventually found the lights and drove round the corner, when this car came right across me and just missed, but I went smack into a block of flats and split my head open. I went to hospital for stitches, but never got breathalysed. To cap it all when I finally got to see Carole she was in bed with her boyfriend. It was one of those days I will never forget! Then I messed the Jaguar up, as I always did with my cars and bought a red mini.

Teenage Ernie 'posing' in Swindon, albeit not necessarily on his own car!

I had a bit of fun in the mini, I had a bet with someone that Carole and I would drive across Coventry naked in it. As I got out of the car, I was trying to put my hands over my 'three-piece suite,' as was Carole. A copper came over to us, he was trying to suppress a smile and asked me, 'Ernie, where are you going?' 'Just for a ride.' He said, 'I would advise you in that case to get on the left-hand side of the road!' Fair play to him, I knew he was dying of laughter.

One evening Carole and I went for a drive and stopped in the countryside. It was pitch black and, as we started making love in a cow field, all of a sudden I gave myself a massive shock on the electric fence, which made me do the dirty deed so quickly Carole said, 'That was a good 'un!' I still haven't paid the farmer the bill for the electric fence!

After Noel Cantwell finished as Coventry's manager, Quinton Young and I met him and Malcolm Allison at the Old Mill for a night out. We had a good evening and inevitably I had too much to drink but still drove. On the way back it was raining hard and, as I drove round a corner in the countryside, I skidded into a tree. I knocked my head against the rear view mirror and split my nose. I was looking from the top of a hill down to Finham, where I used to live, but I couldn't start the car. I knocked on a couple of doors to see if anyone could give us a push but, as it was about two o'clock in the morning, I didn't have any joy. All of a sudden I heard a siren and saw the police park just down the road. Then I heard the police dogs barking, so I ran straight through a hedge and ended up in a ditch full of water. I sat there waiting for the police to finish searching the area, and when they went further up the road I made a dash for it. I knew I couldn't go back to my house, as they would have checked the car with our address, so I went to Noel's house. I used his phone to ring Anne and, as I was speaking to her, I heard the sound of our doorbell on the other end of the line. I told her to tell the police I'd gone away for a few days. Anne told me the police were hiding for me round the corner in the morning, so I laid low for forty-eight hours. The mini was ok. and I got away with it that time.

One year I went to a place in the middle of the countryside for Coventry's Christmas party – why I drove I do not know. After the meal we arranged to go to the house of one of the girls who worked in the office. On the way I took the wrong turning, stopped and asked Quinton, who was with me again, 'Am I all right behind?' 'Yes.' I reversed and all of a sudden found myself driving backwards down a hill, just missed a tree and went into a river. We both sat in the car with the water up to my waist and being a non-swimmer I was starting to get worried. 'We're in a river,' Quinton said. I replied, 'You said it was alright behind.' Quinton said, 'Well I couldn't see the river, could I!' We managed to get out of the mini through the window, staggered up the hill and I phoned Harold Smith, who got someone to tow it out of the river. We went to this girl's house, we didn't want to miss out, although we had dirt all over us, mud from the river and our clothes were soaking wet! We carried on with the do and when I got home my missus said, 'I never heard your car pull up.' I replied, 'I left it at the party just to be safe.' While I was training the next day Anne got a phone call to say they'd got the mini out of the river. The mini still worked, but I got a lot of stick for that – the boys said, 'Have you still got your amphibious car?'

My next car was a Triumph Herald Estate while I was still at Coventry, which I kept for several years before I got another red mini. Then I had a type of jeep for a while; I felt I needed a tank by then but I bought the next best thing. After that I had a white Vauxhall van, which I was driving one windy night when the window blew out next to Carole. Carole went mad at the bloke I bought it from. Then I got another white van, they were cheap and seemed good runners, but what did I know about cars? After that I bought a diesel Peugeot, which was cheap to run. I had so many problems with my cars that in the end one of my mates in Gloucester, Neil Whitehead, used to come out driving his car behind me in case mine stalled!

My first drink-driving conviction was in 1968 when I was at Coventry and driving up to see Carole. It was a Sunday and on the way I stopped the car to watch a game of football. Someone reported me and I got breathalysed. On the Monday I had to see Noel Cantwell and expected an almighty bollocking. He asked what I was doing and it really surprised me when all he said was, 'That's all right.' Noel used to live round the back of me and a few days later Anne went round their place to see Noel's wife Maggie. When she came back she told me Noel had recently been breathalysed in London driving the wrong way up a one-way street. So it all became clear why he didn't give me a bollocking! He never said to me, 'I know how it feels,' but he did offer to get me a solicitor.

Driving ban number two happened when I played for Doncaster at Southport in 1973. I drove up and met one of the Kay sisters after the game. I spent the evening with her and stayed the night at Maurice Setters' place. I fell asleep driving back, accidentally ran into the back of a car, which I wrote off and got banned for three years. This was about seven in the morning, so I still had alcohol in my body – I was ok but tired. I'd been paid £800 so far for Doncaster and the cost of compensation and my fine added up to £860!

One day in the late 1980s Jim and I had been out window cleaning when I was doing it part time and we stopped for a few drinks. Jim drove me back to Ledbury from Gloucester and was driving very erratically. Just before we got home we stopped at a phone box, where I rang Anne to let her know I was nearly home. I went for a pee and when I got back Jim was sitting in the passenger seat, so I got into the driver's seat. The police were waiting for me – someone must have reported us and I took the blame – I didn't even drive off. Even at court Jim said he was driving, but they didn't believe him and ban number three took me off the road for another three years.

Ban number four was when I was working in the commercial department of Swindon. I was living in Ledbury, but actually staying with Keith Morgan that particular week. I was asked out to the country pub in Ogbourne of a Swindon supporter. It was his birthday, I took a lady with me and stayed there the evening. I had a few drinks, nothing excessive and was told that, as it was out in the sticks, there wouldn't be any police there. I got into the car at the end of the evening, drove a couple of yards out of the car park and the police flagged me down. Someone must have stitched me up. Jim Hickman, who was my solicitor, is a mad Wolves fan and has somehow managed to get lighter sentences for me over the years. He thought I might have gone down for this one. When I appeared in court I noticed the main magistrate of three started winking at me. I looked behind me as I thought he was winking at someone else. I pleaded guilty, was banned for another three years and fined £300. Jim thought I was lucky. I asked him who the magistrate was and when he mentioned his name, I realized it was our family doctor! I hadn't seen him for such a long time I didn't recognize him. He shouldn't really have been on the bench that day, as he knew me, so I think I was very lucky.

Ban number five was when I was driving while I was already banned, it was four months before it was due to run off. I needed to go and help someone as usual in Gloucester, when the police spotted me. I was fined £200 and got three points on my licence – I think I was again pretty lucky it wasn't worse.

I've been done six times and have run all of them off apart from the latest one in June 2003, when I thought I had finished but was three weeks short of the previous ban. I went out to help a young lass who lived near us in Gloucester look after her kids. I stayed up all night at her place and drank a bottle of vodka, as I was in a lot of pain with my hip at the time. At eleven o'clock the following morning I drove the kids down to the river to feed the ducks. On the way back I was stopped as one of the kids was jumping up and down on the back seat, was breathalysed and arrested. I should have been jailed as I was well over the limit, but when it went to court and I explained the circumstances they fined me £50 and gave me another two-and-a-half-year ban, but if I went to a special driving course they said it would be reduced by six months. Virtually every time I got banned I'd been trying to help someone.

I started drinking when I was thirteen and worked in my mate's pub, my dad and mum didn't know. I had about six pints of beer one day when I was fourteen, and that put me off for a long time when I was ill. I started seriously drinking when I went to Coventry. There were some fairly heavy drinkers already there and I fell into that culture, because it was a lovely atmosphere. I've always drunk shorts, I've never been a beer man, probably because of my experience at fourteen. I never let it interfere with my football though, I very rarely drank after Wednesday. I wouldn't have wanted to jeopardize my career. I know I still like a drink and like to think I can keep it under control. I like a bit of fun, but I also know when to stop drinking.

In our twelve rounds of life, attention and its ultimate sporting manifestation, adulation, is a reward many footballers crave. When it goes there is no substitute, no shape to the day, no banter with the lads at training, nobody chanting your name – the soundtrack of life no longer roars. Ernie has been left with no assets but plenty of memories. He has latterly been on a losing run at life's casino, but this is no time to make trenchant judgements about his lifestyle.

I enjoyed every minute of my career and only felt low if I couldn't play. I lost count of the number of times the club doctors gave me painkillers or cortisone

2004 – Ernie and Carole.

injections, which have led to arthritis, especially in my knees. I would always try to have a bit of fun on and off the pitch when it was the right time to do it. I played it hard and fair and with a smile on my face. Perhaps I could have gone a bit further in my career, but I've never been serious in my life and I'm not about to change now!

Ernie's name at all his clubs remains timeless. Perhaps the last word should be reserved for the lady of the house, wife Carole who says of her husband, 'I love Ernie out of my head, he is the loveliest person in the whole world. He is my kindred soul and puts up with everything and everyone. Before I met him he wasn't animal-orientated, now he puts up with everything I like. Everybody from the neighbourhood pops by to see Ernie, he's got such a kind nature. I've gone though all his suffering, his hip replacements, and wouldn't swap him for the world.'

Fourteen
Tributes to Ernie

SWINDON TOWN

Bill Atkins

Ernie was on the ground staff when I joined Swindon, but I missed out on fully seeing his potential, as when I was eighteen I went into the Army for two years to do my National Service. We worked on the council when I came out. He'd drive down my road, which was a cul-de-sac, at all hours and annoy the neighbours in this dumper truck – I don't know how he managed to get hold of it in the evening.

He was a pretty good goalscorer, very strong for his height, with a low centre of gravity which made it difficult for people to knock him over. He had strong legs and was very determined. I remember him battling against people like John Charles, six foot plus, yet off the field I can't remember him getting into any bother. He played just behind me in midfield and got a lot of balls out to Mike Summerbee and Don Rogers, who put the crosses in for me and Jack Smith. Ernie was always on hand to pick up any loose balls round the edge of the penalty area, where he scored a lot of his goals from. He was such a good striker of the ball, apart from with his left foot!

We all went out training once and when we got back, everybody's shoes had been nailed to the wooden floor in the dressing room – we think we knew who it was! When we went on our training runs of about six miles, Ernie was always the first home, but we knew he was the worst trainer. He used to get this old boy to give him a lift in his van and the only people who didn't know what was happening were the manager and the trainer! He stood at the end saying, 'Second again.' There was a great camaraderie and the younger players mixed with the more experienced ones like Sam Burton, who was a great goalkeeper and Maurice Owen, who was a legend. It was a great atmosphere and we had so much fun, we were always laughing. It was a joy to go in to work, it didn't feel like a job. The team spirit was among the best I experienced in my career and everybody got on really well together. I think Maurice influenced Ernie on

165

and off the field – off the field he encouraged him and told him that, if he got his head together, he would be a very good player. On the field Maurice was very, 'Let's do the job, let's do it right.'

Not knowing anybody when I first joined Swindon, Ernie's mum and dad often invited me round for tea which I really appreciated. Ernie's dad was brilliant, he was very laid back and reminded me of Arthur Haynes, nothing worried him. When I first came out of the Army I was living in digs, then I got married and so did Ernie, but we were still mates. We both had the same car, a little A35 and when petrol was about five bob a gallon, Ernie would buy half a gallon as he was usually skint. I said to him, 'How far do you think half a crown of petrol is going to get you?' I have thousands of friends from football, but only four real mates – Ernie is one of them.

Sam Burton

Bert Head told me to go down to the recreation ground at Rodbourne to keep an eye on this young lad playing schoolboy football. I followed Ernie around for quite a while and told Bert that I thought he was worth a chance. I never remember Ernie have a stinker, he was a wonderfully gifted player and hit the ball beautifully. If he was playing today, I've no doubt the way he struck the ball would be compared with David Beckham. There was nothing swanky about him, he was just a nice lad. Mike Summerbee was a good 'un as well, but Ernie stood out. Whenever we played Bristol City, Ernie was the one young player they knew they had to watch as if he had a chance, he would score. I think he made his name with his performances against City.

When he first came to the club Ernie was a very quiet lad, he hadn't travelled much, so we took it upon ourselves to educate him. We were always having a bit of a laugh, but did nothing to hurt anybody. When we travelled away, as a youngster Ernie came with us to gain experience. We stopped in hotels and Ernie's table etiquette wasn't great. With three or four knives and forks either side of the plate, Ernie didn't know what they were for and we always put him on the wrong road for a bit of a laugh. We were in a classy hotel once when I told the waiter that Ernie kept saying it was margarine on the table, not butter. He said indignantly, 'Oh no sir', he was most upset. We were staying once at Ashby-de-la-Zouch and spotted an old van outside the hotel. Maurice and I found a pair of wellington boots and put them underneath the wheels of the van, so you could see them sticking out. We told Ernie that someone was stuck underneath and he had to lift the van up, as we were both carrying injuries. He was getting panicky when we told him he had to do it! There was a monkey in the back garden of the hotel and we told him if you gave him a drink of lemonade it would bring him luck for the game. There was Ernie throwing lemonade at it!

We sat one day at the table messing about in a big hotel, when Bert Head stood up and said, 'Ernie, keep away from Maurice and Sam, I told you they'll get you into trouble,' but he stayed with us all the time. We weren't regimental like some clubs, it was like a big family and created an excellent team spirit. I pinched his socks one day and he'd walk around town with no socks on. I nailed his shoes to the bench another day, but he'd never blame me or Maurice, he'd always blame someone else.

I was teaching Maurice how to play golf once when the ball went through the window of the office and Bert Davies, the secretary, came out showered with glass. The next day we bought an American steel helmet and gave it to him.

When Ernie started cutting hair, we had a sign printed and stuck it on his bedroom door, 'Haircuts by appointment.' Ernie said, 'That's very kind of you.' He thought we were doing it as a favour, but we were having a bit of fun. He cut my hair regularly and was actually quite good – I have a photo of him doing my son's first haircut. He loved us taking the mickey and loved messing about with us.

We got back to the ground one day after an away game. After all the rest of the players had dispersed Maurice put this barrier across the exit of the car park. With Mike Summerbee as a passenger Ernie drove his mini under the barrier up to the windscreen. It wedged it and flattened his bonnet right down to the engine! Maurice and I never owned up to that one as Ernie was trying to claim off the council. One day we took his A35 and drove it into the goal. We all lifted it up and turned it sideways between the goal posts so he couldn't move it out. The groundsman was used to our antics by then. Another time Maurice and I tied his bike on the flagpole and pulled it up to the top of the pole! He bought a caravan once but it only lasted a few days, as he ripped the side of it off when he hit the curb and it toppled over. He didn't care – once we knew what had happened we kept on asking if he was enjoying his caravan weekends.

He used to call round window cleaning at my house and on one occasion when he went to lunch I put his ladders up a tree. When he came back he couldn't find them and said to me, 'Sam, you've pinched my ladders!' One day I was doing some cementing and kept putting cement on the window just as Ernie thought he'd finished cleaning them!

Peter Chamberlain

I was with Swindon Town reserves when Ernie appeared on the scene. We used to watch the schoolboys play in the morning and I saw this fifteen-year-old squat kid. He was the image of Wayne Rooney, strong and aggressive and I thought he was going to be some player. He was all right foot with loads of ability, magnificent control, a great passer of the ball and courageous. He was also hard and knew how to look after himself – at an early age he could dish it out. Bert Head treated all the players the same regardless of personality. There were a couple of youngsters called Malcolm Harvey and Keith Colsell with outstanding potential, but as they were sensitive lads they didn't make it, while Ernie was always a strong character and was absolutely revered at Swindon.

When he was working for Arnold Darcy and myself during the summer, we went one lunchtime to a café in Chippenham and sat wearing our overalls at a table close to this guy, who was eating a salad. As we were waiting for our meal, Ernie said in a loud voice, 'I'm not having a salad again today, with all those caterpillars we found in there.' It was priceless watching this guy rifling through his salad!

My family are all rabid Evertonians and I was transferred to Aldershot the day before we played Everton in the FA Cup. Everton were a wonderful side then and murdered us. Bobby Woodruff or Keith Morgan threw the ball to the near post and Ernie would stand and flick it on across the goal. It was almost impossible to defend – he was so strong people couldn't get to him and it produced a lot of goals. In the cup-tie Everton posted a man in front of him and Bert reputedly told the players afterwards, 'That bloody Chamberlain told Everton about that!' Of course I had no contact with them.

We opened the innings playing cricket for Swindon. I don't remember him being a particularly good cricketer, but he had a good eye and would have been good at any sport as he was a natural ball-player. I was not in the same class as Ernie – for me he was a genius but I don't think he fulfilled his potential as he was often played out of position. He played outside right or centre forward, but his position was midfield, as he had vision and was a natural. If he'd played consistently in midfield, I'm sure he would have played for England. He's always been a friendly, easy-going lad, would go about with anyone, and is a lovely, lovely man.

Dave Corbett

I come from near Chippenham and went to Swindon through Geoff Fox, who used to play for Bristol Rovers. In those days there were no ground staff at the club, so I left home and Town gave me an apprenticeship at British Rail. I was a fitter, turner and erector on steam engines and while working there met Ernie's dad. He worked on the traversing, where they used to take the steam engines and move them up and down the tracks. I can't remember the technical name, but Ernie's dad was in charge of the traversing machine. He was a very friendly, cheerful chap and got to know me, as I played for Town reserves. He was into football and I came to realize Ernie was very much like his father.

I was a part-time footballer on four or five pounds a week and got into the first team when I was about eighteen. It was a full-time job at BR and whenever there was a midweek game, I used to have time off to travel, play, then had to be in to work the next day. It was quite hard work, but I enjoyed it. My apprenticeship lasted five years until I was twenty-one, when I went full-time at Town and left BR. As part-timers we used to train on Tuesday and Thursday evenings under the lights. I'm four years older than Ernie and I think he filtered in with our training when he came on the books. I remember as a youngster he had good ball control and was broad, so he could shield the ball well and was hard to knock off the ball. Anyone who knew anything about football could see he was a very skilful player and an outstanding prospect.

All the youngsters came along at the same time, they slotted in and it didn't bother me as they were good players. You're only as good as your last game and at least I had a trade to fall back on. Mike Summerbee came down, was very fast and strong and eventually edged me out of the team. There was no animosity from me when Mike took my place, I was quite happy and didn't ask to be transferred but Ellis Stuttard, the Swindon trainer, moved to Plymouth as manager and asked me to go there. I left in 1962 when I was nearly twenty-two, Ernie was only eighteen but had already established himself in the team.

Arnold Darcy
Ernie was a gifted young player, a natural, and very powerfully built for a young kid. He was stocky and strong, with great ball control and a presence you don't seem to see nowadays. If he got the ball at his feet, there was no moving him and he had the ability to play it on from there. He was a brilliant volleyer, a clean hitter of what was then a heavy ball. He was consistent every week and would take all the free-kicks and penalties. Walt Bingley used to take the dead balls including penalties, but he wasn't completely sure about taking them. Ernie had that confidence, he didn't seem to have any nerves, whatever the occasion. He was like a little lad and his natural ability got him through.

As a young lad he was full of mischief, always pulling tricks on everybody, a confident kid without being cocky. I think he got a lot of his humour from Sam Burton and you immediately took to him. We'd finish training and have a bath, a big bath where all eleven of us could get in. We'd put a substance like a black bubble bath into the bath. One day Ernie put about a gallon of it in and the bubbles went out of the bath, all over the dressing room, down the players' entrance and virtually on to the pitch – typical Ernie! Even in the dressing room, when we would be getting changed before a match, you'd lose a stocking or a boot and knew Ernie was about. We were nervous, but Ernie would start talking like he was just going to the pictures. That sort of temperament was a great asset to a young player, it must have saved him a lot of nervous energy.

Keith Morgan

As a young lad Ernie was brilliant with the ball and a star from the beginning. He was far better than the average youngster, particularly in his thinking. We used to play head tennis in training and everyone wanted to be on his side as he was a brilliant juggler and it was Ernie versus the rest. I've seen the ball come to him and he'd flick it round his marker with great skill. He was superb in hitting the ball in the air and came up with some very good goals. I remember one against Northampton Town (March 1965), when he scored a brilliant volley into the top right-hand corner. I've seen Ernie hit one of those old leather balls round the wall into the net, which was very difficult in those days. He was like the old-style inside forward, give him the ball and he could hold it for ten minutes. As he matured he got to know when to hold the ball and when to pass it and he worked well with Mike Summerbee, they were a good combination.

The Shrewsbury game in 1963 when we won promotion could have gone either way. They were our bogey side and Arthur Rowley came round afterwards and shook our hands. The crowd was on the pitch at the end and everybody was lifted onto the fans' shoulders. It was a fantastic evening, as we were all still young, having grown up together. We all went out together, the first team, reserves and 'A' team, all forty of us including our wives and girlfriends, which helped the team spirit. We all trained together as well and the younger players learned from the first-team players. If the reserves played we all went and stood behind the Town goal, if the 'A' team played we all watched them at Shrivenham Road. When I was on the ground staff, you had to look after five players. You'd clean their boots and get their shirts and tracksuits ready, and if you didn't you got a clip round the ear. At the end of the week you got two shillings and it was a good discipline.

Ernie used to have a Vauxhall 37, an enormous gangster-like car, he could hardly see over the wheel. It had the big headlights and you lifted up the bonnet from the side, concertina style, but it leaked oil all the time. We all used to go to Bill's Café in Swindon town centre after training and when Ernie stopped he would put a white china pot under the car where the oil was leaking. When we left he would take it up and pour the oil back in the engine or forget about it and drive off, leaving this pot lying in the middle of the road. He was accident prone, especially in his cars. When Swindon put up a new fence around the car park, before the cement was dry Ernie had backed up into one of the posts and knocked it over!

Ralph Owen (brother of Maurice)

Maurice was a fatherly figure to all the young players, but with Ernie it really seemed like a father and son relationship. Ernie absolutely idolized Maurice, he used to watch him from the Stratton Bank end when he was ten years old and his one ambition was to walk on the same football pitch as Maurice. Maurice knew Ernie was a complete footballer – 'There's nothing you can teach him,' he said. Maurice thought that Fred Coleman took a lot of credit for the young players that came through to play for the club. I remember Ellis Stuttard said to me, 'With Sam Burton in goal, George Hudson at centre half and Maurice centre forward, we've got the experience down the middle, the youngsters can carry them,' which they did.

Maurice and Sam were the instigators of any mischief. Maurice would load the gun, Sam would fire it and Ernie would back them up. When Sam visited Ernie's pub once, as he saw him come though the door he nailed down every single ashtray so he wouldn't nick any! Ernie was very quick-witted – I remember he was once asked in an interview, 'Any more of your family play football?' Ernie answered, 'No, but I've got a lodger who thinks he can.' Of course that was Mike Summerbee! Ernie shook hands with Danny Williams once when he had an electric joke in the palm of his hand and Danny jumped eight feet in the air.

Maurice was a Chindit in Indian Malaya towards the end of the Second World War. Arsenal were very interested in signing him at one time after coming down to play Swindon in a friendly. Leslie Compton was marking him and said, 'Cheerio Maurice, hope to see you at Highbury.' The Arsenal manager Tom Whittaker even looked into his character, but Maurice wouldn't push himself. He wouldn't have received any more money anyway because he was already on the maximum wage of £20 per week. Wolves were also interested in him and offered £14,000, but Maurice was happy and settled at Swindon.

Stanley Matthews was scheduled to play in Maurice's testimonial, but was injured in an exhibition game the weekend before and couldn't make it. He encouraged Maurice to use his name to pull the crowd in – it was the England side.

Maurice was very easy-going, very placid, but suffered for about twelve years with Alzheimer's. It was probably as a result of so much heading of the old leather ball with laces. His long-term memory wasn't too bad, but his short-term memory suffered. Maurice's wife Marjorie nursed him through his illness and I can confirm there is more than one Mother Teresa around. Ernie still speaks to me regularly and is a real gentleman, Maurice really took him to his heart.

Bobby Woodruff
Ernie and I were very close and grew up together, being local lads and we had some very good times. Ernie was best man at my wedding and his first wife Anne was our only bridesmaid. Anne was from Swindon and my wife was from the other side of Marlborough so, if we were playing at home, after the game we would meet at the Wheatsheaf in Ogbourne, just outside Swindon. It was a

racing pub, Sir Gordon Richards had a stable there and we got friendly with the jockeys. We were young lads and had some good fun, but we also took our football seriously.

After the big defeat against Port Vale in 1960, on the Monday there was an inquest. They didn't want any of the youngsters in the team meeting, we played our socks off and didn't have any idea the game was crooked. I remember getting our own back early the next season, when we beat Port Vale 6-0 and I got a hat-trick. It was only when Bert was struggling for players that he picked me up front.

I also scored three for Wolves against Sunderland before Ernie came, all headers, when we won 3-0, and played up front later in my career for Cardiff. There wasn't the pressure on me to score goals, as I could always fall back into midfield. When Ernie signed for Wolves, I played up front in the Southampton game which he watched, as we were struggling. By half-time I'd scored and we were 3-1 up. In the second half we had a nightmare defensively and conceded eight goals. The following week there was one change, they dropped me and put Ernie in. I couldn't believe it, they kept the same defence, so I went in for a transfer. I didn't hold it against Ernie, but as far as Wolves were concerned that was more or less it. We did play some games together, like when we beat Portsmouth 8-2 (November 1965) and I scored a couple. Off the field we were in our prime at Wolves – we used to get rid of the wives for the weekend and carried on where we'd left off at Swindon!

WOLVERHAMPTON WANDERERS

Mike Bailey
I had played against Ernie when I was at Charlton and met him for the first time when we were both selected for the England Under-23 side. We shared a room together but didn't sleep that night, as we got on so well we sat talking about football. The next time I saw him was when Charlton went to Wolves and I popped in to have a chat. Things went a step further when Ronnie Allen, who had been player-manager at Crystal Palace, signed me. Ronnie had seen me play just along the road at Charlton, but Ernie certainly put a word in for me at Wolves and that was a big factor in the move.

The way we played together at Wolves was telepathic, we just hit it off. Ernie was very strong, quick off the mark, had a really good touch and his movement was always so good. You knew if you passed it to him, he wouldn't give it away. I knew I could link up with him, he played very simple football and was a dangerous striker. Most of his goals were getting an angle past his defender and cracking them in.

He was one of these intelligent players who broke off into areas where defenders didn't know whether to pick him up or stay and defend. You knew the ball was going to be safe at his feet and he would release it when you were ready. Ernie was like the classic old inside forward, very clever, he timed his runs well and was a quality player, one of the best I've ever played with.

We just missed out on promotion the first year, but we all wanted it so badly we worked really hard the next season. Huddersfield were one of the big teams and we played three games over Easter (1967), beat them twice 1-0 and also beat Hull, which virtually clinched promotion for us. The Bury game was where all the emotions broke out, we were tearful and so pleased that we had made it to the First Division, where we felt we could push on from. Derek Dougan was another big factor, he was a huge signing for us and we had some very good players.

Ernie and I bought houses near to each other and our wives became friendly as well. We socialized together, became very close friends and went to the games together by car. My wife used to work in Birmingham and one evening when we were playing Cardiff City, I had to pick her up. Coming back the traffic was terrible and we got to our house at 7.05 p.m. for a 7.30 p.m. kick-off. I automatically thought Ernie had gone to the ground, but he stayed for me. We reached Molineux just in time, dashed in, got changed, and beat them 7-1. We were let off as the performance was so good, but it was typical of Ernie not to let anybody down.

We even bought our cars at the same time, as we thought we would get a better deal if we bought the same ones together. I remember they were two soft-top MGB's, he bought a red one, I had a blue one. We were advised by our accountant to buy the Savoury Duck restaurant together in Birmingham. It had a caravan burger-bar to go with it on another site, but when Ernie was transferred to Everton we sold it. It was quite an experience!

I was very disappointed when Ernie went to Everton and couldn't understand why the club wanted to transfer such a good player. It certainly affected my own performance and took me a while to adjust, as we were such good friends. I knew exactly what his runs were, what he was going to do and he knew my game. We didn't see each other for a while, but when I was player-manager at Hereford, I couldn't make the training session a couple of times and called him at his pub at Ledbury. I asked him if he could take the training, the lads enjoyed it and he did a good job for me. He was unbelievable, funny all the time, always mucking about, absolutely brilliant, and was a shining light in my life.

Fred Davies

Wolves didn't buy a lot of players in those days and when they did, they had to be of the right type. Ernie settled in well and had good feet, he was a good player in a high standard of football. You could not have met three more lively characters than Ernie, Waggy and Terry Wharton. When they returned from Las Vegas during the summer tour in 1967, they came back with Clint Walker's autograph and I said, "How the hell did you get that?" I didn't go there as we had been travelling about a lot and it was the first time we'd had a few days off. It was one of those decisions I wish I'd have done with hindsight, but I finally made it there last year thirty-six years later. Its always nice to see Ernie, he was always a bubbly character, but he didn't cut my hair, I never let him near it!

Derek Dougan
Ernie was a straightforward inside forward who became a midfield player. He wasn't an out-and-out striker, but he had powerful strength, a good shot on him with the ability to score goals. Ernie was very effective, he and Denis Law were doing bicycle kicks, overhead kicks and volleys thirty-five years ago. I only played 11 games at the end of the 1966/67 season and was blessed with 9 goals. With 20 goals from 37 games, Ernie also had a good ratio of goals to games. He was always capable of scoring a goal or two when they were needed, and the game that stands out for me was at Preston towards the end of that season, when Ernie scored both goals in a 2-1 win that virtually clinched promotion.

I joined Wolves in March 1968 and Ernie left about six months later. I could never really understand why Wolves sold him, although Ronnie Allen was a good wheeler-dealer in the transfer market. He bought me for £50,000 and I know he could have sold me to at least two clubs for £80-90,000. People are tempted to get a couple of years out of a player and, if they can double the price, view that as a good business deal, and Ronnie was the sort of guy who could see a doubling of his money with Ernie. After Ernie was transferred I went through a barren patch and put pressure on Ronnie to give me a bit of help up front. In the end he went out and bought Frank Wignall, a big strong fellow, who did a good job in the short term.

Ernie had a gorgeous West Country accent, Dave Burnside took him off better than anyone else. He was a funny guy, you never saw him down in the dumps or moody. In the dressing room you always need two or three funny guys and at Wolves there were a number of outrageous guys, including Ernie. After my first training session with the club, I heard two or three of the lads say, 'Ernie, all right for a haircut?' I thought this was the usual dressing room banter, but next thing I knew out came the scissors and comb, and Ernie was cutting short back and sides. I just couldn't believe it – it was the only time in a twenty-five year career I ever saw that!

Phil Parkes
I was only a kid when Ernie came to the club, but I could see he was a great player. He could hold it up and get people into the game, had good vision and

was very strong. I played one game when Fred Davies was injured, then after we won promotion we went to America for nine weeks, which is a long way away from home. That's where I got to know Ernie, who kept everybody happy and was the life and soul of the party – still is! He's a great friend and I still see him now, he's still the same and hasn't changed a bit. He's a bit partial to a wig nowadays, as he hasn't got much hair, which is ironic as he used to cut all our hair! We did a 'Questions and Answers' session with Stevie Bull one evening and Ernie took over, the audience were eating out of his hand. That was Ernie.

Bobby Thomson
I first came across Ernie when we played together for the England Under-23s in Romania. We were youngsters trying to achieve our dream of playing at the highest level for the full England side. Ernie was a quality player and you knew when you played the ball up to him, he was always going to hold it up for you or lay it off to someone else. I personally think he was more effective coming from deep as a midfield player, and he was always up and down. He tried different things when he was at Wolves, so it was no surprise to me when he scored the 'donkey' free-kick. When we were at Molineux last year, Ernie had a great reception from the supporters. When he got home at two o'clock in the morning, he phoned me up and said, 'I've just got back in, we've had a great day, haven't we?' What a character, he was very good for the dressing room and there aren't many like that in the game nowadays.

Dave Wagstaffe
My first recollection of Ernie was when he turned up in the dressing room with his West Country accent, which was a bit strange to me, coming from Manchester. He sounded like a Wurzel! He was a thick-set lad, had good vision and got up there in the box with an eye for the goals. Playing wide on the left I linked up a lot with Ernie and we worked well together. We all lived on the same estate and went out together. When he moved to Everton I moved into his club house, which was bigger than the one I had. He cut my hair occasionally, we used to go down to a barber's called Jim and Syd, where he helped them out cutting hair at the shop for a bit of fun.

We had some good times together and I shared a room with him in the sixties. When we toured America in 1967 I just happened to meet Davy Jones while we were there. We lived in the same area in Manchester and all the kids knocked about together. He organized a trip round the studios, when they were recording a show. He also took Ernie, myself and Terry Wharton to Lenny's Boot Parlour in Los Angeles, which was next to Colombia Studios. He said we could have what we wanted and he would foot the bill, so he bought us a load of clothes. We met this chap outside the Coliseum before one game who nobody knew, but we immediately recognized as Tommy Steele. We took him in as a player and he watched the game from the bench. After one match Ernie and I decided not to go back to the hotel on the bus, but walked out of the stadium to find a bar. We wandered into the Bronx area and had to be rescued by the police, who drove us home. They told us we shouldn't have been in that area, they actually said we shouldn't have been alive!

We were in Switzerland on another tour one year and I shared a room with Ernie and Joe Wilson. It was the first time we had seen a minibar in the room of a hotel. Joe said very sternly to us, 'That's the first thing you don't touch!' In the morning he told us he'd ordered breakfast. There was a knock on the door and room service brought in three glasses of sherry and three eggs. Joe broke the eggs into the sherry and made us drink it – it was vile. We had a game that evening too, when Joe lost his rag with the referee and bawled at him. His false teeth fell out – he had forgotten to leave them in the dressing room!

Terry Wharton

Ernie was always fun, a players' player, a very entertaining bloke, and a big influence on my game. The biggest thing he did for me was win penalties, I never missed one in my career and Ernie won me quite a few. Under Stan Cullis it was 'Run, run, run, get fit, you wingers get down that line and cross the ball.' The big fellas came in to convert the crosses, like Ted Farmer, Ray Crawford and Jimmy Murray. It was all training, hard work, but you never got a pat on the back, even if you scored three against (West Bromwich) Albion, which I did. Stan would say, 'Keep your feet on the ground son, I don't want you driving cars at your age,' which was nineteen – dreadful. Then Ronnie Allen came and changed the situation completely. He brought in Ernie, Mike Bailey and John Holsgrove, and it became short and quick stuff, and five-a-side. We'd get the ball, flick it up and work on ball skills, it was a big change. It was lovely for me as before he came I used to do fourteen laps round Aldersley Stadium before we started training. Whether or not it did us any good, I don't know, but we got promotion when everybody played superbly and, for an inside forward, Ernie scored a lot of goals.

I've never seen anybody as good as when the ball was played up to Ernie with his back to goal. There's not many like that in the modern game, where the ball never leaves you, Ruud Van Nistelrooy is the nearest I can think of. He was one of the best players I ever saw shielding the ball, especially round the box. He'd lay it off to me, Waggy or Doog, it was magic. You just couldn't get it or knock him off the ball. He turned on a sixpence and defenders couldn't cope with it. That's where he got a lot of his penalties from. He wasn't like a Peter Broadbent, who dragged it back and sprayed balls about, he was a different type of player.

We became very close friends and had a brilliant time when we went to Las Vegas with a couple of friends. We went to Ann Margret's ball at the Riviera Hotel. Ernie kissed her hand as she came out and we were going in – she didn't have a clue who he was! Before a game Ernie always put his top on first in the dressing room and nothing else, so that everything was left hanging out! When he came up last year for a Wolves dinner, we got to bed at six o'clock in the morning. He was up after an hour's sleep before going back to Gloucester. Typical Ernie.

EVERTON

Alan Ball

I remember Ernie as a player at Swindon and always thought he had a lot of ability. He lived near me and Howard Kendall at Freshfields. I don't know why Harry Catterick played him wide, we all knew his best position was down the middle, where you could hit him with the ball and it would stick. I think Harry brought him in to bolster his squad. Harry worked him hard as he thought Ernie was overweight, but he wasn't, he was as fit as anyone, it was because of the way he was built. Harry used to take him for extra fitness training, which we laughed about, but there wasn't an ounce of surplus flesh on him. Then he got that great free-kick against us for Coventry. I was in the Everton team that day and it was talked about for a long, long time.

We used to have fun all the time and he was always playing practical jokes on us. He loved wearing big, hairy hands when he was driving and used to wave at the old ladies across the road. I remember him standing with a big gorilla suit he put on some days just for the craic and he was always up to pranks like that. One day he came in wearing a 'Sergeant Bilko' head with the glasses, and made Howard Kendall and I wear one as well. On our way to training we used to drive past these workmen, who were Liverpool supporters, digging a big hole. They'd wait for us every day and give us plenty of stick. Every Friday we got some eggs from Norman Bodell, the physio. On our way back from training one Friday, when the hole had got deeper and you could barely see the workers from the top, Ernie said, 'Pull over.' He got out of the car and battered them with these eggs, and got back into the car laughing his head off. That was type of thing he was up to every day. I used to ring him up and ask if he could babysit for us. He'd say, 'No problem, I'll get the Louis suit out.' He'd turn up dressed in his 'Louis' gown, a big dressing gown that made him look like Joe Louis when he went into the ring. He would always do you a favour if he could and was great fun. He was wonderful company and I had a fabulous time with him.

Howard Kendall

As Ernie was a stocky player, I think Everton tried to make him fitter and slim him down. They would bring him back in the afternoons for circuit training, but Ernie was suited to the build that he was, not what they tried to make him. He lost some strength as a direct result, which may have affected his game. It was wrong to try and change him, as you sign a player for what he's got, not what you want him to be.

Alan Ball and I lived close-by to Ernie and we shared a lift to the ground. He had a soft-top MGB and one day, when it was his turn to take us into training, he stopped at a garage to get some petrol. The attendant came out and Ernie said, '50p's worth please.' It must have been a Thursday, which was wages day, as all we had on us was fifty pence!

Of course he scored that goal against us when he was at Coventry. I remember it well, as I was in the wall. When Ernie was working with children, he came up to Everton with all the kids and I was happy to support him. It was typical of Ernie to think of taking them there for the day, he would do anything to help. Ernie was a tremendous character and everyone at the club loved him.

Brian Labone

I first met Ernie when we played together for England in Bucharest against Rumania Under-23s. Then I came across him when we played Swindon in the FA Cup (1963). They had a great forward line of Summerbee and Rogers, plus Ernie and a fella called Smith at centre forward. It was played on a frozen pitch and they were expected to give us a bit of a fight, but we turned them over 5-1. I suppose Harry Catterick must have noted him from then on and we played Wolves in a couple of FA Cup games (February 1967) and were a bit lucky to win after a replay. They had a useful side and Gordon West made a tremendous save from Ernie in one of the games.

While he wasn't a failure at Everton, he was among the big boys when we had a pretty good side and it was unfortunate he never quite made it for some reason, as he was a good player. We had the famous midfield trio (Ball, Harvey and Kendall), so you had to be very good to displace them. It wasn't his fault he was played out wide, it was just circumstance and the formidable opposition he had to compete with at the time. Perhaps Harry thought he could have done a useful job for Everton, perhaps he bought him as a good back-up, but he was wasted on the wing. Mind you some managers bought players so that they couldn't play for anyone else – put them on the bench and frighten the opposition!

He was very direct, small and nippy, well-built physically, brave and with a good right foot. He was short and built like a little tank with bandy legs, not fast over a long distance, but quick in short bursts over twenty yards. I had a phone call one day from Noel Cantwell, who asked me about Ernie. I told him he hadn't quite made it here, but he was a battler and fighter, and would do a good job at Coventry. He needed a regular first-team place and then it rebounded on me when he scored that goal against us, so he owes me a favour! He was a funny lad with his West Country drawl, a bit of a country yokel, but was a great character and I'm sure with his accent Westy (Gordon West) will have given him some stick.

Alex Young
When Ernie came to Everton he had a sports car – the lads thought he must have got a good signing-on fee! He was a strong, powerful player, a real worker in the middle of the park and gave 100 per cent all the time. At the time I played with him, as I remember I played wide right, maybe it didn't always look like that, and Ernie played in a midfield role on the right side. Maybe he was told to play wide right but being a midfield/striker, perhaps Ernie drifted inside. With Alan Ball, Howard Kendall and Colin Harvey around in midfield, it would have been difficult for him to get in the side on the right-hand side, especially as Bally was the best midfielder in the country at that time.

He was a smashing lad off the park, the lads took to him straight away, as he was so funny. He used to have a gorilla mask and a big hairy hand with paws on it. He would stop his car at a bus stop in Liverpool, ask the way, then stick this big gorilla hand out to shake hands with them. Norman Bodell used to come round to Belleview and offer us double-yolk eggs. Ernie would have a dozen and throw them out of the window of his car at passers-by. The police came to the training ground to warn the manager someone from the club was throwing eggs with a gorilla mask on – it had to be Ernie!

COVENTRY CITY

Dietmar Bruck
I made my debut for Coventry City against Swindon on the last day of the 1960/61 season in the old Third Division, when we were both youngsters. Ernie scored the only goal of the game, so I knew early on what a good player he was. I played against him for quite a few seasons after that, but was an inside forward at the time, so didn't come into direct contact with him. Perhaps he kept clear of me because of my reputation!

Ernie was a fantastic asset to the Coventry side. We needed a player with his talent and skill, as we were struggling to stay in the top League, and he had the added experience of having played in the First Division. He was strong, with good movement off the ball and had that extra bit of skill when he controlled the ball and created openings for his teammates. His attitude was first-class and some of his first-time lay-offs were tremendous. He played some great one-two's with Willie Carr, they were good friends off the pitch and that obviously helped their understanding.

We practised the donkey free-kick at training but it didn't go to plan at all, with most of Ernie's volleys going over the bar. On the actual day against Everton we had a free-kick from twenty-five yards out on the left side of the pitch. Willie was standing by the ball and I was ready for him to push it to one side, so I could have a crack at it. I was standing behind Ernie when he said, 'Let's try what we worked on in training.' I said, 'You must be joking, you haven't hit the target yet.' I was still waiting to be set up when they decided between them to flick the ball in the air, bang, and that was it. Being right behind them I knew as soon as Ernie hit the ball, it was going into the net. It was a brilliant goal and a shame that something so skilful was outlawed.

We played at Newcastle one evening when I was just coming back from injury and was on the bench. We had a good result and afterwards myself, Ernie and some of the lads went out for a few drinks. When we got back Ernie and I stayed up talking until about four in the morning. When we eventually got up for breakfast Noel Cantwell collared me. He wanted me to get my kit and play in a reserve match at Sheffield that evening – it wasn't the best preparation. Thanks Ernie!

Noel said he wanted us to take the American tour seriously, but it all went wrong from the start as on the plane we all got a bit pissed. We flew in from New York to Rochester and as I had about forty relatives in Buffalo, I asked for time off to visit them. Noel declined but I said sod it and off I went. It's true Ernie and Neil Martin tried to cover up for me, but in the end we all got fined and were suspended for the next game. We were away for a month and visited about twelve states, but there was a great team spirit and we had a superb time. Ernie was a real character in the days when there were some around and was always in the thick of things.

Willie Carr

Ernie was the type of footballer I enjoyed playing with. I knew every time I played the ball up to him, he would never mis-control it. He was very clever as well, I used to make a lot of forward runs and he would just flick the ball into my path without me having to break stride. He is still the best front man I ever played with. I remember a volley he scored against West Brom (August 1971). He was at the far end of the eighteen-yard box and I just picked him out, and he volleyed it back into the far corner of the net. He was very skilful and the best volleyer I ever saw. Kenny Hibbitt at Wolves was a similar player to him, who also suited my style of play.

The donkey free-kick was from about twenty yards out and it was set up to try in the Everton match after we had practised it a few times. Dave Clements was also beside us and I actually flicked the ball up too high. You could see Dave shaping up but Ernie put out an arm and let go. Another great goal he scored was against Burnley (April 1971), when I played the ball to him and he obviously had a quick look before chipping it over Tony Waiters from almost the halfway line.

I remember we played in a charity match once when Ernie went down and they brought a stretcher on to carry him off. It must have been set up, but with Ernie around there's never a dull moment and I love him to death.

Chris Cattlin
Ernie and I signed on the same day for Coventry and stayed in the Hotel Leofric. On our debut we beat Manchester United with Best, Law and Charlton in their side. It was a fantastic win and, while I got the headlines that day, we all played well and it was a wonderful result for the club. It looked like we were going down, but I think me and Huntie helped them stay up, otherwise it might have been a very brief stay in the First Division.

Huntie said we'd have a couple of drinks in the hotel to celebrate the United win. I wasn't a drinking man, coming from a professional sporting family. My dad was a professional footballer and I thought if I went out for a pint on a Tuesday, I was being a real devil. Ernie said to me, 'These liqueur pale ales won't affect you, Cat.' I thought they were lemonades and we started talking football. The bar was used for the tactical board and the bottles, which were the players, started moving along the bar as the tactics came out. I didn't realise what I'd been drinking until I got up to go to the toilet and both the bolts came out of my neck! I knew I was in big trouble and had to go straight to bed, that was my real introduction to Ernie. When it came to training Ernie was first-class, but a night out early in the week was fine. I was the young upstart from Huddersfield and Ernie put his arm around my shoulder and took me under his wing. Along with George Curtis, he helped me through my early days at Coventry, which I needed and appreciated, and was very professional.

He was a very gifted footballer, you could sling a ball to Ernie at any height and he could instantly control it. It never bounced off him and I can't think of anyone in the game who has the wonderful control Ernie had. He scored many great goals, in particular volleys, he was a great volleyer of the ball and we took it for granted he was going to hit the target.

Ernie was a top-class guy, great for the dressing room and a laugh a minute if you could understand what he was saying. He was a fantastic character and had a wonderful personality. We had some characters in the dressing room in those days, like Maurice Setters and Neil Martin. Mick Coop and I were the youngsters of the side and, coming from Huddersfield, it was a complete education for me.

When we went on tour to Barbados, the drinks were very expensive over there, so George Curtis said, 'We'll get a bar and I'm in charge of it.' George went deep-sea fishing one day, and Ernie and Maurice Setters broke into the bar. We were playing bottles on the beach, where you place these bottles as far away as possible and come back on them to where you started. Ernie fell on one of the bottles and split his nose just as George appeared, so we all legged it. I was rooming with George, he came in and said to me, 'Who's broken into the bar?' I said, 'What bar?' and he gave me a couple of whacks for not telling him. He spotted blood on the ground and followed it along the corridor to Huntie's room, where he gave Huntie and Maurice a good hiding! George took it personally as he thought they were winding him up.

Ernie was a very talented, underestimated player and brought a lot to the club and dressing room. The pressure didn't get to him at all whatever the occasion and I've got the utmost respect for him, as he was a wonderful player. In fact, if he had a bit more pace, which is what you need at international level, he would have played for England.

Mick Coop

Ernie joined soon after Maurice Setters and, with Chris Cattlin, their experience kept us in the First Division during a difficult time, when Noel Cantwell was new to management. I was just a young man when Ernie joined Coventry, having made my debut in the Second Division in 1965. I was the youngest member of the team, so I looked to experienced professionals like Ernie to direct me. He was full of fun and enlightened my life on a number of subjects! Looking back it was refreshing to be involved in the game and a wonderful time for me.

It was a good atmosphere at the club and we had a lot of fun. At that time there were quite a few players like Ernie who liked a drink, and for me it was an experience and an eye-opener. I was a young person who didn't get involved in the drinking and antics that went on, as I was trying to make my way in the game. I don't know about the match-fixing allegations, I never knew anything about it.

Ernie was a character, you don't find them in the game now. He wasn't necessarily the most professional or most mobile of players, he did things the way he wanted to, but he was a very effective player and made a great contribution. Of course the donkey free-kick will never be forgotten, it was brilliantly executed. Ernie is a lovely, jovial person, who wouldn't harm anybody.

George Curtis
I first remember Ernie when he played for Wolves and we beat them 3-1, which virtually guaranteed promotion for us from the old Second Division. There were over 51,000 supporters in the ground, a record, as they sat along the touchline, and the ref said it would be okay as long as they didn't run on to the pitch. It was one of the best games I've played in and one of the personal highlights of my career.

Then I broke my leg in the second game of the First Division at Nottingham Forest and was out for over six months, so I didn't play with Ernie a lot to start with. He was a good player who could score goals, although he wasn't big enough to be a good header of the ball. He was very quick over a short distance and was always there looking to score, so had a good quota of goals. He was a character, great for the dressing room and we became very good friends.

Ian Gibson
Ernie was a very good player and if you ran he knew when to give you the ball – with some other players you made the run but the ball never came. You knew what he was going to do – people thought he was slow but he wasn't, he had that five to ten-yard burst of speed and was on the end of something before anyone realized. You put the ball across and Ernie was in, he was a good anticipator. When we beat Tottenham 3-2 (December 1969), Ernie and I kept the ball for about the last five minutes in the corner flag. I remember Jimmy Greaves came over and tried to kick us. I jumped out of the way and tapped him on the head, he didn't like that. We used to have competitions with Norman Pilgrim and Jimmy Andrews in training to try and hit the crossbar from the edge of the penalty area. Ernie and I could do it when we wanted, Jimmy Andrews was good, but Norman, however much he tried, never got close, bless him. Every Monday morning Ernie, Maurice Setters, Bill Glazier and myself had to get weighed in. Ernie soon told me that if you got someone to hold the weight at the bottom with two hands, it knocked off about four pounds!

Bill Glazier
Ernie was a wonderful footballer, a ball-player, he had all the tricks. He wasn't a tackler, but he was a wonderful dribbler and player of the ball. He wasn't really a midfield player, more like the old inside forward. As a goalkeeper he was an outlet to aim for, if we were winning he could get the ball down the corner and hold on to it, which took a bit of pressure off the defence. With Maurice Setters and Neil Martin, a little group of us had a few drinks together and Noel Cantwell joined in as well. Ernie was always in on everything, from drinking to playing cards on the bus – he was always having a craic.

I was also with Ernie in the England Under-23 squad. Alf Ramsey spoke with his upper lip and I remember him pointing to the blackboard saying, 'One does this and this is how one does that.' Of course Ernie piped up, 'What does one do if somebody else gets the ball?' He was always taking the piss out of Ramsey and was a wonderful character to have in the dressing room.

Joe Mercer – written in 1974

My old pal Ernie is one of the great characters of the game. He was a wonderful boost for team spirit; full of jokes, enjoying his football and everything that went on. My first contact with Ernie was when he was a youngster with Swindon. I was in charge of an England Under-23 touring party and we wanted another forward. So I went down to Swindon to have a look at Ernie and Mike Summerbee and found them digging graves! Ernie was a personality then. We had characters like Alan Mullery, Brian Labone, Fred Pickering, Colin Dobson, Peter Bonetti and George Cohen in the Under-23 side then, but Ernie could out-joke any of them.

He always had loads of ability, loads of skill and few players can volley a ball as well as Ernie. Not long ago I watched him score a spectacular volleyed goal from way out. He gives the ball top-spin when he hits it and not many goalkeepers can stop those. Ernie was also doing his usual – controlling it, coaxing and advising the younger players – and still enjoying his football. He's always had a weight problem, he makes no bones about it – he likes living well. That's part of his make-up – no manager can take that away from him. He's no Olympic sprinter – running isn't one of his strong points, but he does have a burst of acceleration over ten yards. His specialist feat is scoring goals – he gets about one in every three games and that's not a bad record, and he's still banging them in. And in the dressing room he's great for morale. Nothing is ever so grim, no defeat is such a catastrophe as all that, if Ernie Hunt is there.

Derrick Robins (ex-chairman)

A super chap. We were very pleased to have him in the Coventry team and he was a very skilful player. One thing that stands out in my mind was when the team was on holiday in Barbados and Coventry City played Barbados. As you would know, there was only to be one result and we were playing exhibition football. We were leading 3-0 when Ernie decided to give an exhibition of ball control from his foot, around his neck, over his back, through his legs and so on. This exhibition lasted at least three minutes, maybe four, during which time, to everyone's astonishment they all stopped playing the match and stood in silence watching this superb display.

Maurice Setters

Ernie was a talented lad with a footballing brain, not very quick but an excellent passer of the ball. He was good at making himself available so, as a defender playing behind him, I got hold of the ball and played it to him. He scored some terrific goals with free-kicks, as he could bend the ball in the way they do now, so I think he would do brilliantly today. It was the quality and experience of players like Ernie that Noel Cantwell brought there, that helped Coventry survive. I remember the last match of the (1967/68) season against Southampton, it was a very big game and we couldn't afford to lose. I had to do my job, which was to mark Ron Davies, who was flying a bit at that stage, but all the other lads contributed and played well.

I fancied him to come and do a job for us at Doncaster when I was manager and he did well for me. At one time Doncaster had big gates, but we were struggling when I went there and we had to redevelop the club and try to bring the crowds back. Ernie was still a big name in football and helped turn us round and attract the customers back.

He was a jolly, likeable lad, who never had a bad word in him. One of his great attributes was that he was good off the pitch and in the dressing room, and everybody appreciated him. I was always one of the back runners with Ernie at cross-country. Now and again we might have found a short cut – it was all part and parcel of the fun we had.

BRISTOL CITY

Paul Cheesley

Ernie was coming towards the end of his career when he joined City and most pros will obviously remember him for the free-kick as it was so inventive and it also worked on the day, which was even better. He was pretty consistent, mainly playing wide for City, although he never had the pace of a gazelle. He also played up front with me on a couple of occasions and with his first touch was good on the ball. He was a bit of a target man, not one for the ball over the top, but with his strength he held people off and got people into the game.

As strikers we were always asked to chase the full-backs down the line, so when the ball was with the opposition 'keeper you split wide. On one particular occasion when the ball was back with the 'keeper, it was Ernie's turn. He chased towards the full-back and Alan Dicks shouted at him, 'Ernie, get after him.' With Ernie's bandy legs he got there in the end and just reached the full-back, who knocked the ball up the line. Ernie took his standing leg away, which made it look twice as bad as it was. The referee came up to him and said, 'Ernie, I'm booking you for a late tackle.' Ernie replied, 'I got there as fast as I could!'

Another time Ernie made a tackle and this guy was on his hands and knees. Ernie got on top of him like he was mounting a horse and started slapping his arse – his antics were so funny.

At that time his arrival was great for morale as we were struggling a bit, but he cheered us up and made it fun to go to work. He played a big part in every aspect of the club and if you were down in the dumps he would pick you up, that's the kind of character he was. He was charismatic and funny all the time, and I'm proud to have known the man.

Bryan Drysdale

Ernie was just a character and was very funny. He never seemed to be serious about anything, we got on well and had a lot of fun together. He was still a wonderful player when he came to the club. There were a lot of youngsters in the side and his experience was invaluable for them. He played on the left side and for me, as a left-back, he was a tremendous target and it was good for me to have him as an outlet. We had some exceptional players at the time and a very good team spirit, particularly with Ernie around.

We deserved to beat Leeds in the cup replay. We really got at them, it was a tremendous result and we had a few beers afterwards. It can't be coincidence that we had such a good cup run soon after Ernie joined us. I remember the karaoke affair, when we sang in Greece at a holiday camp on an end of season tour. We just got up for the craic. I think the trip was perhaps a reward for the cup run.

Gerry Gow

Ernie had a lot of skill, he was a strong boy and a very good player, who made a big difference to our side. It was at a time when Bristol City were bringing through a lot of younger players, who hadn't reached the level Ernie had played at. It gave us that extra bit of experience and Ernie was the sort of person who youngsters need to play alongside to learn to play the game. A lot of the FA Cup run was down to Ernie and his experience, as most of the players had never been that far. Every year some team from the lower division, perhaps not doing too well in the League, seems to have a good cup run and 1974 was our turn. We were the first team in the country to beat Leeds that year and pulled off one of the biggest surprises in the cup for years. Getting the draw at Ashton Gate was a big bonus for us, but no-one could have dreamt we would have gone to Elland Road and beaten them with the side they had at the time. It was the biggest game of my career up to that time.

I used to room with Ernie and remember waking up with a hell of a hangover in Greece, covered in chocolate ice-cream. In Cyprus I woke up next to a six-foot plant in bed with a little white hat on and a pair of sunglasses – Ernie was without doubt behind that as well. We were all fit lads and trained hard but we also drank hard, not like now when everything is geared to fitness. When Ernie took his clothes off to go in the bath after training, he certainly frightened a few of the boys!

Tom Ritchie

Alan Dicks bought Ernie as a stabilizing influence, as we were a very young outfit when he came to us. Obviously everyone associated Ernie with his Coventry days and that free-kick, and the younger players like myself were a bit starry-eyed at first, but he was a great bloke to have around. As a young lad growing up there, you would sit in the dressing room and try and take it all in. He could talk seriously about the game, which the younger players listened to intently, but with his sense of humour he was a real comic off the pitch and a lovely man.

The one game I do remember was the FA Cup-tie at Hereford, which was a very difficult place to go to at the best of times, especially a cup tie. When we got to Edgar Street the pitch was like a bog. Ernie went into a sliding tackle and must have gone on for at least thirty yards and ended off the pitch. He stood up and was covered from head to toe with mud and you just had to laugh at him. We won the game 1-0 and it was the start of our cup run. On that day Ernie did a hell of a job for us and I'm sure he guided us through that. I think Ernie played a big part in the cup run, he had the experience of playing against the big teams. We had come up through the youth team together and, with an average age of about twenty-one, he added that element of stability. Playing wide on the left he did a great job for us, although I don't think it was his favourite position. Looking back he was the right man for the job and had that effect on and off the pitch, a guiding influence and deadly serious on the pitch, but always comical off it.

Ernie couldn't swim and on holiday the lads remember him treading water by putting his hands out as though he were swimming. It was an absolutely amazing stroke and you could see Ernie do that. He was a great lad, a lovely man and I thoroughly enjoyed my time with him.

Gerry Sweeney

When Ernie came to Bristol he made a big impact on and off the pitch. He was a character, liked a laugh and was tremendous in the dressing room. He took the mick out of us Scottish lads, but we had a great bunch of boys and he slotted straight in. He was always up to tricks and pranks, he was a livewire, but in the dressing room everyone could give it and take it, and he gave us a lift. He used to say I took things too seriously, which I probably did, but I had to work harder at my game than Ernie, who was a natural. He used to tell me to calm down and relax and enjoy it a bit more, as I was always uptight.

On the pitch he was a playmaker, he brought others into play, had quick feet and a good brain. He was sharp over a short run, was very good with both feet, but didn't like the hard slog of training. Ernie had a positive effect on the youngsters, who had already been together for a few years and his experience rubbed off on other people, like Gerry Gow, Trevor Tainton and Tom Ritchie, and they blossomed.

During the season of our cup run, we didn't do brilliantly in the League, but we seemed to play better away from home. Some supporters suggested we stay away before the cup games at home, so we stayed at Chepstow. When we played Leeds we gave ourselves forty minutes to get to the ground and ended up arriving about half an hour before kick-off – Leeds arrived before us! Billy Bremner scored a great goal for them, but we kept plugging away and Keith Fear lobbed the 'keeper for the equalizer. We played the replay on a Wednesday afternoon because of the miners strike. We were up for it even more, as we had nothing to lose after a creditable result from the Saturday, so we gave it a right go. Another Gerry Gow move led to our goal from Don Gillies and it was a great result. The draw had been made before the game, with the winners to play Liverpool. Bill Shankly had already assumed Leeds would win and said what a great game it was likely to be. He came in after the Liverpool game and apologized for that and congratulated us on our victory over Leeds. Before the Liverpool game the whole team stayed in Chepstow again and we got to the ground even later. There was such a big crowd we had to have a police escort in the end to get us safely there.

Alan Hawks

I was just a semi-professional footballer and was invited on the Rhodesia trip in 1973, as I had my coaching licence. The rest were all full-time pros and ex-pros, so when I got on the aeroplane at Heathrow I went to the back as I didn't know anyone. I must have dropped asleep and woke up when I felt this wet finger stuck in my ear. That's how Ernie introduced himself and we've been friendly ever since. We had a terrific time and myself, Roger Hunt and Ernie went around together a lot.

We met this young lady one day in a country club, who invited us for a game of squash. Ernie and I had never played the game before but Roger had, so he took her on first while Ernie and I watched from the balcony overlooking the court. When Ernie went on he did quite well, as he was a natural at any sport. On about the third point the girl hit the ball against the front wall and it bounced to the back of court. Ernie hit it short and she went forward to return it at the front of the court, so Ernie was standing behind her. Without her noticing Ernie dropped his shorts exposing his considerable assets, but this girl had no idea what was going on. He pulled his shorts up just in time to carry on the rally! We nearly fell off the balcony and the girl couldn't understand what we were laughing about.

When I visited him at his pub once, there was a builder working on a brick fire grate that went from floor to ceiling. We had a few vodkas together in another room and halfway through the afternoon heard this almighty crash. We rushed in and the chimney had collapsed on this fella, all you could see was his leg and head sticking out of the rubble. That was the type of thing that could only happen to Ernie!

Ernie is the most generous bloke you ever will meet, which is probably the main reason why he hasn't got any money now – he would give you the shirt off his back. He is a genuine bloke and a very gentle man.

Jimmy Greaves – written in 1981
Ernie was a confident, chirpy character on and off the pitch, with an enthusiastic approach to football and life in general. His inventive mind is shown in the 'donkey' free-kick. He was a great pro, who was particularly adept at shielding the ball and laying it off, regardless of what merciless defenders were doing to the backs of his legs in the days when they were allowed to tackle from behind.

Appendix: Career Statistics

Swindon Town 1959-1965 – 239 appearances, 88 goals (in brackets)

	League	FA Cup	League Cup
1959/60	16 (3)	3	–
1960/61	46 (14)	3 (3)	3
1961/62	41 (18)	2	2
1962/63	43 (24)	4 (3)	2
1963/64	34 (12)	1	3
1964/65	29 (11)	1	1
1965/66	5	–	–

Wolverhampton Wanderers 1965-1967 – 82 appearances, 35 goals.

	League	FA Cup	League Cup
1965/66	31 (10)	3 (2)	–
1966/67	37 (20)	4 (1)	1
1967/68	6 (2)	–	–

Everton 1967/68 – 16 appearances, 3 goals.

	League	FA Cup	League Cup
1967/68	14 (3)	1	1

Coventry City 1968-1973 – 168 appearances, 50 goals.

	League	FA Cup	League Cup	Fairs Cup
1967/68	7 (1)	–	–	–
1968/69	39 (11)	2	5 (2)	–
1969/70	31 (9)	2	1	–
1970/71	31 (10)	1 (1)	4 (1)	4 (1)
1971/72	27 (12)	2	1	–
1972/73	7 (2)	–	–	–
1973/74	4	–	–	–

Doncaster Rovers 1973 (on loan) – 9 appearances, 1 goal.

	League
1972/73	9 (1)

Bristol City 1974 – 16 appearances, 2 goals.

	League	FA Cup
1973/74	11 (2)	4
1974/75	1	–

Bibliography

Publications

Brown, Jim, *Coventry City, The Elite Era* (Desert Island Books, 1998)
Ponting, Ivan, *Everton Player by Player* (Guinness Publishing, 1992)

Newspapers

Birmingham Sports Argus
Coventry Evening Telegraph
Coventry Observer
Swindon Evening Advertiser
Western Daily Mail
The Times

Other Sources

Brown, Jim, Historian of Coventry City Football Club
Hughes, Graham, Historian of Wolverhampton Wanderers
Lock, Gordon, Memorabilia Officer of Everton Football Club
Mattick, Dick, Historian of Swindon Town Football Club

If you are interested in purchasing
other books published by Tempus, or in case you have
difficulty finding any Tempus books in your local bookshop,
you can also place orders directly through our website

www.tempus-publishing.com